EVERYDAY LIFE IN

Colonial America

A universal preoccupation with religion, courage, ingenuity, and a great capacity for hard work characterized colonial Americans. There was no leisure time as we know it, no labor-saving devices, no radio, no means for rapid transportation or communication. It was a time when an idle brain and idle hands were sinful.

Dr. Wright records with vividness and accuracy the history of the period in terms of the average American, from down on the farm to the founding of the great universities, from deviltry on the holidays to the beginnings of the exploration of the West.

Old Bruton Church, Virginia
at the time of Lord Dunmore.
Oil on canvas, 18x27⅛ inches.
A. W. Thompson, 1840-1896.
Courtesy, The Metropolitan Museum of Art,
Gift of Mrs. A. Wordsworth Thompson, 1899

EVERYDAY LIFE IN
Colonial America

BY LOUIS B. WRIGHT

LIFE IN AMERICA

G. P. PUTNAM'S SONS, NEW YORK

EVERYDAY LIFE IN AMERICA SERIES

Everyday Life in Colonial America
By Louis B. Wright

Everyday Life on the American Frontier
By Louis B. Wright

Everyday Life in the Age of Enterprise
By Robert H. Walker

Everyday Life in Twentieth Century America
By John W. Dodds

Seventh Impression

© 1965 by Louis B. Wright
All Rights Reserved
Published simultaneously in the Dominion of
Canada by Longmans Canada Limited, Toronto
Library of Congress Catalog Card Number: 65-28484
PRINTED IN THE UNITED STATES OF AMERICA
12216
SBN: 399-20057-6

Contents

Acknowledgments

The author and the publisher are indebted to many institutions for permission to use illustrations in their custody. For help in finding illustrations, we wish particularly to thank the staffs of the Folger Shakespeare Library, the Henry Huntington Library and Art Gallery, the Henry Francis du Pont Winterthur Museum, Colonial Williamsburg, Inc., the Shelburne Museum, Old Sturbridge Village, and the New York State Historical Association.

For aid in research and in the preparation of the manuscript for publication, the author is deeply in the debt of Mrs. Elaine Fowler of the Folger Shakespeare Library staff. Her ingenuity has saved him many hours of labor and her judgment concerning material of interest to young people has been particularly useful. The author is also under a continuing obligation to Miss Virginia LaMar of the editorial staff of the Folger Shakespeare Library for expert technical assistance.

LIFE IN  AMERICA

Edited by Louis B. Wright

EVERYDAY LIFE IN
Colonial America

BY LOUIS B. WRIGHT

Preface

An understanding of the distant backgrounds of the American people is essential to a clear comprehension of the life that we have developed in modern times in the United States. We often think of history as the chronicle of wars and treaties, of laws debated and passed, of abstract matters that have no relation to what went on from day to day in any given time and place. We forget the significance of the normal routine of men and women who lived and breathed in a definite time and a definite place. Their reactions to the events of their times provide the substance of history, and we would do well to try to discover what everyday life was like in any given period.

The purpose of this series is to give a brief account, not of the great political movements of the times, but of the normal way of life of the American people. This particular volume attempts to show what life was like when our ancestors were trying to gain a foothold on the Atlantic seaboard in the seventeenth and eighteenth centuries when we were still a part of the rising British Empire.

In a brief treatment we have necessarily had to omit many details and to pass lightly over some events that may arouse the interest of readers to seek further information. A suggested reading list is appended for those who wish to pursue some topic at greater length.

L.B.W.

The fight for America was waged by sea and by land, against Spaniards, Frenchmen, Hollanders, and Indians. *From the Folger Library copy of Theodor de Bry,* America, *Part III (1605).*

1

The Beginning of the
American Dream

Even before Englishmen had made a permanent settlement in the New World, the mysterious land across the
ocean held a promise of adventure and of an infinite number of good things for those with the courage to seek them.
Men young and old had heard tales brought back by seamen who had sailed down the coast of Africa, skirted the
Canary and Madeira islands, touched the coast of the
Spanish Main, and perhaps found their way into the colder
waters of the North Atlantic. Long before Sir Walter Raleigh dreamed of a colony in Virginia, English sailors had
been probing the western seas and learning about the riches
that Spaniards had already discovered in the New World.
Stories of the gold that Hernando Cortez had found in the
land of the Aztecs in Mexico and that Francisco Pizarro
and his brothers had taken from the Incas in Peru filtered
into England and stirred imaginations, until every appren-

13

Stories of Spanish loot from the lands of Montezuma and the Incas stirred English imaginations and courage to dare the unknown. *From the Folger Library copy of Theodor de Bry,* America, *Part V (1595).*

tice in London and every lad who watched the ships sail out of Bristol and Plymouth harbors dreamed of discovering wealth in some adventure overseas.

During the early years of Queen Elizabeth's reign, John Hawkins, a member of a notable trading and seafaring family, had made several voyages to the African coast, where he had bought or captured slaves and traded for "elephants' teeth," or ivory. He had taken his cargoes to the Spanish possessions in America, where English traders were forbidden to go, and had exchanged his slaves for sugar, pearls, and gold, which brought him a handsome profit. With Hawkins' third expedition, in 1567–68, went a young man named Francis Drake, destined to become one of the most famous of Elizabethan seamen.

This expedition met disaster at San Juan de Ulúa, a tiny port fifteen miles south of Vera Cruz on the Mexican coast. There Hawkins fortified an island and planned to defend it against marauders while he engaged in contraband trade with Spanish settlers on the mainland, who were glad enough to buy his slaves and pay in gold. Unhappily for Hawkins and Drake, a Spanish fleet bringing the new viceroy of Mexico arrived at the port and demanded entry. Fearing to antagonize Spain by defying the viceroy, Hawkins exacted a guarantee of safety and allowed the Spanish flotilla to anchor in the harbor. Once secure inside the haven, the Spaniards treacherously attacked the English ships; they left Hawkins and Drake with only two serviceable vessels, in one of which, the *Judith*, Drake sailed away.

Hawkins, with more than two hundred men in the *Minion*, was forced to put half of them ashore. Of the hundred men Hawkins left in Mexico, three eventually found their way to the North Atlantic coast, where they were rescued.

London in the days when every apprentice dreamed of sailing down the Thames to adventure in the New World. *From the Folger Library copy of Visscher's* View of London, *ca. 1616*.

Sir Francis Drake, *El Draque* to Spaniards, was the first Englishman to complete the circumnavigation of the world and the first of England's great naval heroes. *From the Humphrey Dyson collection of Elizabethan proclamations in the Folger Library (1618).*

These three told such an incredible tale of their adventure, of the lions and tigers encountered along the way, that few believed they could have survived the long trek north.

The Spaniards' treacherous attack on Hawkins and Drake at San Juan de Ulúa left Francis Drake with a bitter memory. Henceforth he was an inveterate enemy of Spain —a crusader determined to do as much damage as possible to Spanish shipping, to take as much gold as he could from Spanish sources.

Between 1571 and 1573, Drake made three attempts to capture mule trains laden with gold from Peru that came overland to Nombre de Dios on the Isthmus of Panama. Frustrated at first, he at last captured such a quantity of gold and silver bars that his men could barely stagger down to his ships under the burden of treasure. Nevertheless they managed to load enough precious metal to give each member of the crew a substantial sum in prize money when

Drake reached Plymouth in August, 1573. Sailors boasting of their wealth, flaunting Spanish gold in the face of land-lubbers, soon made Drake's exploit known throughout the port towns of England. When other captains set sail for the Spanish Main, crews were not hard to find.

Drake had only begun his career of harassing Spain. Before he was through, his name would be a terror in Spanish households, and Spanish mothers would quiet their children by threatening them with *El Draco,* "the Dragon." Drake's most famous expedition was his circumnavigation of the globe in 1577–80, when he fell on the unsuspecting Spaniards on the west coast of America, robbed their towns, captured their ships, and loaded his vessel, the *Golden Hind,* so heavily with treasure that she was in danger of foundering.

On this voyage, Drake explored the west coast of the

Drake's exploits on the Spanish Main were the favorite topics of gossip in English port towns and an effective substitute for recruiting posters. *From the Folger Library copy of Theodor de Bry,* America, *Part V (1595).*

A map of Drake's circumnavigation by Jodocus Hondius, one of the foremost cartographers of the day. The inset ship is the only known contemporary likeness of the *Golden Hind. From the Folger Library copy of Theodor de Bry,* America, *Part VIII (1599).*

land that would one day be the United States at least as far as Oregon. In June and July, 1579, he hove to, probably in what is now called Drake's Bay, just north of San Francisco, to repair and refit his ship. The Indians swarmed down to stare at the strange white men, the like of whom they had never seen. Drake observed that the Indians particularly enjoyed the psalm-singing of his sailors. After recaulking his vessel, Drake nailed a brass plate to a tree, thus claiming the country, which he christened New Albion, and sailed away. On his return, Queen Elizabeth, to the annoyance of the King of Spain, knighted Drake on the deck of his ship.

From this time onward, depredations on Spanish shipping grew more daring, until Spain in 1588 sent the great Armada against England in an attempt to conquer the troublesome island. English seamanship, combined with Spanish miscalculations and bad luck, brought victory to Queen Elizabeth's seamen. England henceforth could claim a proud place among the great powers of the world. She was also ready to claim a place for herself in the New World.

Even before the victory over the Armada in 1588, Englishmen had tried to plant colonies in America. In 1584 Sir Walter Raleigh sent an exploring expedition to the coast under the command of Philip Amadas and Arthur Barlow. They went ashore in the region of Pamlico and Albemarle sounds and came back with accounts of a fruitful and fertile land. To honor the Queen, Raleigh named the whole territory Virginia. This included what is now North Carolina. A year later Raleigh sent out an expedition of seven vessels under the command of his cousin, Sir Richard Grenville, and planted a colony on Roanoke Island. With this expedition went John White, an artist who painted water colors of the Indians and their activities, and Thomas Harriot, a scientist who wrote a book called *A Brief and True Report of the New Found Land of Virginia* (1588). Harriot's book described the marvelous richness of the country, its fruits and produce, its fish and animals, and its possible minerals. All held the promise of prosperity for

An incident of Drake's round-the-world voyage. American Indians, to whom headgear was significant of status, playfully steal the Admiral's hat. Note ship being careened in background. *From the Folger Library copy of Theodor de Bry, America, Part VIII (1599).*

Elizabeth I, who inspired much of the derring-do in her subjects. Raleigh named Virginia for her and Captain John Smith wrote in his history of the colony: "The most famous, renowned, and ever worthy of all memory, for her courage, learning, judgement, and vertue, Queen Elizabeth." *From the Humphrey Dyson collection of Elizabethan proclamations in the Folger Library (1618).*

settlers. The book was the first of a long line of promotional works designed to induce colonists to go to America. Harriot might be called the grandfather of real-estate promoters in America.

Englishmen were ready to believe almost any story about the good things of America, just as all Europeans, for the next three hundred years, would believe in the new land of opportunity across the seas. Raleigh himself was responsible for tales of fabulous riches to be had for the taking; in 1595 he returned from an expedition up the Orinoco River in Guiana, now Venezuela, and told a story of a mountain of pure gold. The ruler of that country, whom the returning voyagers called *El Dorado*, "the Gilded One," was covered with gold dust. Pearls and diamonds, the sailors reported, could be picked up from the sands of the rivers. Although Raleigh's expedition failed to find all this wealth, Raleigh himself believed in its existence so completely that years later, in 1617, he led another expedition to Guiana. This time fortune was even less kind: he discovered no treasure; his son was killed; and he himself returned to be executed for violating his promise not to attack any Spaniards.

Even before Raleigh's 1595 voyage to Guiana, his projected colony in Virginia had failed. The first group gave up and went home in Sir Francis Drake's fleet, which touched at Roanoke Island in 1586. Another group, sent out by Raleigh the next year, completely disappeared, leaving only the mystery of the "lost colony." What happened to these settlers, no one to this day knows.

But Raleigh's efforts were not altogether in vain. His schemes kept alive the idea of a transplantation of English people overseas; and his seamen brought back one commodity, the white potato, which would eventually transform the eating habits of Europe. Raleigh cultivated the potatoes on his Irish estates and introduced potatoes to Ireland.

Sir Walter Raleigh, courtier, in Armada year. Because all shipping was commandeered to parry the Spanish threat, the relief of Roanoke was delayed and the colony doomed. *Portrait by unknown artist. Courtesy of the National Portrait Gallery, London.*

Ultimately, they became so important that now they are known as Irish potatoes. Raleigh is also credited with introducing tobacco, but it was probably John Hawkins, long before Raleigh, who brought tobacco to England. Raleigh, however, helped to popularize its use, and stories were told of his addiction to smoking. One related that a serving-man, finding him enveloped in smoke, doused him with water to put out the conflagration.

Tobacco quickly became one of the most valued products from America. Although hogsheads of tobacco were less romantic to contemplate than the bars of gold and silver the Spanish conquerors brought back, cargoes of tobacco made more men richer—on both sides of the Atlantic—than did all the gold the Spaniards discovered.

But even before tobacco became an important commodity in international trade, it had acquired an importance to Englishmen and other Europeans as a magic drug, a cure-all for any ailment a man might have, from stomachache to gunshot wounds. A belief persisted that the New World's vegetable, animal, and mineral products would provide cures for all the diseases of the Old World. Ponce de León had dreamed of finding a fountain whose waters would confer eternal youth. Others, less demanding than Ponce de León, did not ask for eternal youth but were ready to believe that American herbs might produce wonder drugs. Tobacco was the first universal wonder drug.

A Spanish doctor, Nicolás Monardes, wrote a book on the marvelous remedies to be found in America. His book, translated into English by a merchant named John Frampton, bore a promising title: *Joyful News out of the New Found World* (1577). The subtitle was specific about the value of the book, which it advertised as describing

The rare and singular virtues of diverse and sundry herbs, trees, oils, plants, and stones, with their applications, as well for physic as chirurgery, the said being well applied bringeth such present remedy for all diseases as may seem altogether incredible, notwithstanding by practice found out to be true.

Arrival of the English in Virginia. "We came to an Ile called Roanoak . . . at the north end was 9 houses, builded with Cedar, fortified round with sharpe trees." Then as now, Hatteras was a graveyard of ships. *From the Huntington Library copy of Theodor de Bry,* America, *Part I (1590).*

Of all the medicinal herbs that Monardes described, tobacco treated the widest range of ailments. He reported that it was good for headache, toothache, rheumatism, pains in the joints, stomachaches of every kind, chilblains, swellings of all kinds, wounds of every description, snake bite, and even bad breath. Tobacco could be smoked, chewed, made into poultices, powdered and rubbed into wounds, steeped as a tea, and rolled into pills. For nearly two centuries after the publication of this book, many people believed tobacco was a remedy for various ailments. Although King James wrote a treatise entitled *A Counterblast to Tobacco* (1604), in which he described the death of a man whose body, when opened, contained a bushel of soot, most writers praised tobacco's curative powers. It was not until our own time that tobacco came to be widely regarded as a hazard.

23

Indian village of Secoton, "as we esteemed 80 leagues from Roanoacke" (see John White's map above).
(A) tomb of chieftains, (B) the place of solemn prayer, (C) ceremonial dance, (D) a feast, (E) tobacco patch, (F) hut for human scarecrow, (G) ripe corn, (H) young corn, (I) pumpkins, (K) communal fire, (L) river, source of water supply. *From the Huntington Library copy of Theodor de Bry,* America, *Part I (1590).*

Among other products that Monardes recommended was sassafras, which, he declared, would cure even more diseases than tobacco. For almost any ailment Monardes recommended sassafras tea, to be drunk hot or cold, sweetened with honey or sugar. Tea was brewed from the roots of the tree or from its bark. It was good for gout, for fevers, for headache, and especially as a tonic for the run-down feeling that everyone experienced in the spring. In Europe the demand for sassafras was for a time insatiable, as everyone turned to sassafras tea as a panacea for every ache and pain. The first cargoes sent back from the little colony at Jamestown, Virginia, were largely of sassafras. In fact, so much sassafras was gathered and shipped to England in the early years of the seventeenth century that the market was glutted and the price dropped precipitately. The notion that sassafras tea is a remedy for spring fever is still current; and in the spring, sassafras roots can be found in the markets of Washington, D.C., and other American cities.

Belief in the good things to be found in America increased as the years passed and as more explorers returned to report soberly on what they had seen. Their sailors were sometimes less sober, and the yarns they spun in the taverns of the port towns won for them reputations as great liars. In an old play called *Eastward Hoe*, performed in 1605, Captain Seagull replies to a question about the riches of Virginia:

I tell thee gold is more plentiful there than copper is with us, and for as much red copper as I can bring, I'll have thrice the weight in gold. Why man, all their dripping pans and their chamber pots are pure gold, and all the chains with which they chain up their streets are massy gold; all the prisoners they take are fettered in gold. And for rubies and diamonds, they go forth on holidays and gather 'em by the seashore to hang on their children's coats . . .

Captain Seagull went on to describe the glories of Virginia as a place where any commoner could enjoy such delicacies as wild boar and venison as freely as Londoners could eat bacon and mutton. This land of opportunity, he explained, was no farther than six weeks' sail—even with a moderate wind. The play was performed two years before the settlement at Jamestown, and Captain Seagull was merely satirizing the tales that promoters were telling about the good things to be found overseas.

The belief that gold could be found almost anywhere in America was one of the lures that induced some of the adventurers to enlist in Captain Christopher Newport's company, which landed in Virginia in May, 1607, and founded Jamestown, the first permanent English settlement in America. Many of the company were gentleman-adventurers, men who had never done a day's work, and they were ill equipped for life in the forest. They had come expecting to find another land of Montezuma; and they dreamed of carrying home a hoard of golden treasure as Cortez had done. They found, instead, only an endless expanse of forest and water to challenge the ingenuity that many of them lacked. But, to the credit of Newport's com-

The Virginia Indians were tattooed to show their tribal allegiance or place of origin—much as we brand cattle. *A* was the mark of allegiance to Wingino, "cheefe lorde of Roanoac." *E*, *F* (worn by the man pictured) and *G* were insignia of individual chief men, equivalent, perhaps, to a coat of arms. *From the Folger Library copy of Theodor de Bry,* America, *Part I (1590).*

pany, they set about establishing themselves on the swampy peninsula that they had chosen as the site for their colony; and, after much suffering and many trials, they laid the foundations of a commonwealth that would persist and grow to greatness.

About the time the colony at Jamestown was being settled, another group under the command of George Popham and Raleigh Gilbert made a settlement on the Kennebec River, which lasted through one miserable winter. Popham and others of the company died; but the survivors built a ship, which they named *Virginia,* and returned to England with a cargo of furs.

Though the colony on the Kennebec failed, the survivors came home to demonstrate a new source of wealth in America: furs that were in great demand, furs that formerly had come only from Russia and the Baltic countries. The Kennebec survivors also brought back to England a report of the enormous quantities of fish with which the northern waters teemed.

An explorer and adventurer who had helped save the little colony at Jamestown in its first year, Captain John Smith, made a voyage to Maine and the coast to the south during the summer and fall of 1614. He had come in search of gold, copper, whales, furs, and fish. Though he found no minerals, and the whales escaped him, he observed immense schools of fish; and in a small boat he and his men probed the coast and traded with the Indians for beaver, marten, and otter skins. Meanwhile, others in his crew were catching and drying codfish. He returned to England with a profitable cargo of fish and furs and wrote a book, *A Description of New England* (1616), which served as propaganda for the new land. This book was a sort of

Sir Walter Raleigh, explorer. His search for El Dorado, like his colony at Roanoke, ended in disaster. Onetime court favorite, he was beheaded by James I in 1618. *From the Folger Library copy of Raleigh's* Judicious and Select Essays *(1650).*

farewell to the gold delusion. Smith pointed out that wealth would come from humbler sources, namely fish, and that if he had his choice of the four quarters of the globe, he would choose New England as a place for a colony. He pointed out that fishing had made Holland rich and that it could bring prosperity to Englishmen. New England, he said, was the country for "men that have great spirits but small means," an observation that thousands of sturdy Englishmen proved correct in the next twenty years.

Fishing and the fur trade would prove, as Smith predicted, the source of prosperity to colonists in America and to English merchants at home. The little band of Pilgrims from Leyden who planted Plymouth colony in 1620–21 and the more numerous group of Puritans who began to settle the region around Massachusetts Bay in 1629 soon learned the value of the fisheries and the fur trade, as well as the promise of prosperity held out by trade. In ships that they themselves built from timbers in their own forests, they developed trade overseas that made New England independent and prosperous.

During the late years of the sixteenth century and the early years of the seventeenth century, many Englishmen, especially young men of ambition, looked upon the New World as a land of opportunity—much as immigrants from all of Europe in the nineteenth century looked upon the United States as the culmination of a dream. Englishmen in those early years were often disappointed and discouraged about conditions at home. Money was hard to earn, prices were high, and periodic depressions added to the difficulties that most young men faced. Under the laws of inheritance, only the eldest son could hope to succeed to his father's estate, and younger sons had to shift for themselves. Queen Elizabeth had no standing army and her navy was recruited largely from the merchant navy whenever a crisis occurred. Hence, the military services did not offer careers to young men, as they did in the nineteenth

Tobacco and sassafras, the first universal wonder drugs, had been advertised by the Spaniards before the English arrived in Virginia. The Indians boiled their drinking water with "saxefras." *From Nicolas Monardes,* Joyful News Out of the New Found World *(1577), Folger Library copy.*

century, when England ruled a great empire. A considerable number of youths could look forward to careers in the Established Church, but not every young man wanted to be a parson. The law promised an honorable career for some, but England was already supplied with a surplus of lawyers and not every youth who entered the Inns of Court could hope to make a living from the legal profession. The practice of medicine had not yet attained the prestige it would acquire in later centuries; the barber still practiced surgery and let the blood of patients who thought they needed this treatment. Many an Elizabethan looked upon doctors as little better than quacks—as indeed they sometimes were.

England was still a country of farms and sheep pastures, and from products of the land came most of the nation's income. But something was happening to the old system of

29

A full-scale reconstruction of the *Susan Constant*, 100-ton flagship of the first permanent English settlers in America. They arrived in 1607 and "planted in a place by them called James Towne, in honour of the King's most excellent Maiestie." Note flags. *Courtesy, Jamestown Foundation of the Commonwealth of Virginia.*

farming that had persisted since the Middle Ages. The demand for English wool was increasing abroad, and English landowners were discovering that they could make more profit from raising sheep than they could from leasing their land to tenant farmers, as had been their custom for untold generations. Strips of land that once had been separate little farms were now enclosed into sheep pastures, and the former tenants were forced to wander across the country in search of jobs that did not exist. The wanderings of dispossessed tenants gave the impression of an overpopulation of unemployed and led writers to urge settlements overseas for the surplus population.

But the picture was not all dark. Business and trade flourished as never before, and many younger sons of the gentry and even of the lesser nobility came up to London and apprenticed themselves to tradesmen or merchants engaged in the overseas trade. That way promised to lead to success, and trade overseas sometimes had the added spice of romantic adventure. Merchants and tradesmen were in a better position than landowners to profit by new conditions in the world. As prices rose because of an influx of precious metal from the Spanish dominions—the beginning of a creeping inflation that we have had ever since—they could pass on increasing costs to the consumers, whereas landowners found it difficult to raise rents beyond their customary rates. Not even the transition to sheep raising saved some landowners from hard times and the verge of bankruptcy.

Although money came more easily to the tradesman and the merchant, the landowner—the country gentleman— continued to hold a position of higher social status. Many merchants who got rich in London hoped to buy land eventually and to establish their families in the country as a first step toward becoming members of the landed gentry. The ownership of land was essential to this rise in the social scale. Land was the key to ultimate social success. But land in England was not always easily acquired. For that reason the limitless acres of America held a new promise, not only of wealth but of prestige. Younger sons, who could never hope to hold land in their own names in England, could by the mere act of emigrating become landed proprietors in Virginia or New England. The land hunger of Englishmen could now be satisfied in the colonies overseas and the way was open for a new prosperity for all classes.

Not all the fabulous myths about America circulated by explorers and seamen proved true. Englishmen never found great hoards of gold and silver; they never discovered fountains of youth or panaceas for all the ills of mankind. But they did learn that the land along the Atlantic seaboard, where Fate had ordained that they should settle, was favorable to men of great spirit, as Captain John Smith had declared. Men of such spirit founded thirteen little colonies that in time became a great nation.

2

A New Life in the Wilderness

An expedition setting out today for Antarctica or for some station on a South Sea island has the advantage of detailed information about the climate and weather conditions at all seasons, and about the products of the country, even if, as in the case of Antarctica, one can find there few living things except fish and penguins. At least the potential visitor to Antarctica knows what to expect. If he is headed for a tropical island, he knows all about the inhabitants, the food crops, the insect pests, the diseases, and the problems of every sort that he is likely to encounter. And now we are studying the surface of the moon in the hope of eventually sending explorers there. But the first English settlers in the New World knew little more about life in America than we now know about the moon.

A few explorers had visited the North American continent and had brought back glowing reports, chiefly be-

Many of the early adventurers were spoiled young aristocrats and few knew what equipment to bring. *From the Folger Library copy of Jacob Cats,* Alle de Wercken *(1657–59).*

cause they had arrived during the summer months. For example, explorers who had sailed along the coast of Maine during July and August were convinced that they had visited a semitropical paradise that would produce oranges, lemons, figs, and even dates—fruits that traders were accustomed to bring back from the Mediterranean countries. They were not aware that when winter settled down over the North Atlantic, the cold would hold the country in an iron vise that would make life hard for anyone, even for an Englishman accustomed to freezing winters. The first English colonists had no exact knowledge of climate, native peoples, products of the soil, or of the hazards to be encountered in the new country such as diseases, dangerous animals, and poisonous snakes.

They had as yet no experience in colonial enterprises. A few Englishmen, it is true, had gone to plantations in Ire-

The palisade of the Indian town of Pomeiooc (see map of Roanoke region, Chapter I). Under Captain John Smith, the Jamestown settlers built similar defenses. *From the Folger Library copy of Theodor de Bry,* America, *Part I (1590).*

land, but that was the limit of English knowledge of settling another country. The Spaniards had long occupied vast areas to the south, in Mexico, and in Central and South America, but Englishmen could not draw on the experience of an enemy nation, and if they could have, that experience would have been of little help in a region so different from Latin America. English colonists had to learn the hard way—by trial and error.

The early colonists also suffered because the promoters of settlements overseas were eager to show the new enterprise in the best light possible and, like modern real-estate promoters, they made the land appear more enticing than actual conditions warranted. After reading the promotion literature, many adventurers believed that they would be certain to find gold or quick riches from some other commodity in the land across the seas. Even the most careful and scientific observers described wonders to make any adventurous young man want to go to America. For example, Thomas Harriot, the mathematician who wrote *A Brief and True Report of the New Found Land of Virginia,* tried to give a sober account of things as he saw them, but he could not restrain his enthusiasm for the opportunities that he believed to exist. After reading his book, it is hard not to believe that practically every good thing either was growing or could be made to grow in the soil of the New World. Harriot wrote:

Seeing therefore the air there is so temperate and wholesome, the soil so fertile and yielding such commodities as I have before mentioned, the voyage also thither to and fro being . . . performed thrice a year with ease and at any season thereof, and the dealing of Sir Walter Raleigh so liberal in large giving and granting land there . . . (the least that he hath granted hath been five hundred acres to a man only for the adventure of his person), I hope there remains no cause whereby the action should be misliked.

Harriot asserted that if colonists would come with enough

G · VEEN

This may be the dish described by Captain John Smith in his *Generall Historie*: "In winter they esteeme it [corn] being boyled with beans for a rare dish they call *Pausarowmena*." *From the Folger Library copy of Theodor de Bry,* America, *Part I (1590).*

"Their manner [of planting] is this. They make a hole in the earth with a sticke, and into it they put foure graines of [corn] and two of beanes. . . . Their women and children do continually keepe it with weeding." *From the Folger Library copy of Theodor de Bry,* America, *Part II (1591).*

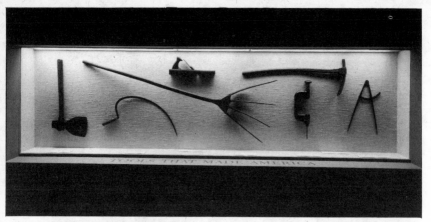

Tools of the early colonists were few and simple. These date from 1750 to 1850 but there had been little change in design in a hundred years. *Courtesy, The Henry Francis du Pont Winterthur Museum, Winterthur, Del.*

equipment and supplies for one year, the country would richly support them thereafter.

The difficulty was that few of the early adventurers knew what equipment to bring and how long supplies would last. The men who made the first permanent settlement at Jamestown in 1607 came without adequate equipment. An ill-assorted lot, they lacked the adaptability and ingenuity that American frontiersmen later developed. Many were spoiled young aristocrats who had not learned to do any useful work. Instead of cutting trees and building houses and fortifications against the savages, they preferred to wander off in search of gold mines. When Captain John Smith gained control, he organized wood-chopping details, put some to planting corn and vegetable patches, and started others to building palisades around their huts to keep out the Indians. But even the discipline prescribed by Smith could not make experienced pioneers of untrained adventurers, and they nearly perished before they learned to adapt themselves to frontier conditions.

Compared with the equipment and supplies that a mod-ern expedition to a primitive country can command, the provisions that seventeenth-century settlers could bring with them were poor and scanty indeed. The voyage required two or three months, though occasionally a ship made it in six weeks. Consequently, only foodstuffs that would not spoil could be brought: hard ship biscuit, dried peas, salt beef and salt pork, flour and grain. Many times, weevils got into the food; or water, leaking into the ships' holds, ruined the stores. Every ship carried its supply of beer as a necessary help against scurvy, but on many voyages the heat of the tropics soured the beer. One of the hardships that the early settlers complained of was the necessity of drinking water instead of beer. Harriot declared, however, that the settlers on Roanoke Island took Indian corn and "made of the same . . . some malt whereof was brewed as good ale as was to be desired." This is the first recorded effort of Englishmen to make an alcoholic beverage from corn. On landing, colonists, wherever they were, had to learn to eat such food as they could procure from the country. For instance, Englishmen who had al-

Why the colonists were afraid to hunt. "To make the noch of his arrow he hath the tooth of a Beaver, set in a stick, wherewith he grateth it by degrees." *From the Folger Library copy of Theodor de Bry,* America, *Part I (1590).*

ways regarded wheat bread as the staff of life had to learn to live on corn bread. The Jamestown settlers would have starved if they had not been able to buy corn from the Indians, grind it into meal, and bake it into corn pone. They may not have enjoyed corn bread at first, but they soon learned that Indian corn provided many different dishes that were nourishing and sustaining.

Tools and implements essential to a modern expedition were utterly unknown to seventeenth-century colonists. They had no power saws, no earth-moving equipment, no trucks and cranes, and, at first, not even a horse or cart. They had their bare hands, a few axes, handsaws, adzes, wedges, mauls, picks, shovels, and hoes. With these implements they had to fell trees, shape timbers for their houses, rive clapboards and shingles, and erect their buildings. They knew how to dig clay and mold brick, and very early they made enough brick for a few structures. The amount of human toil required to establish themselves is hard for us even to imagine today. But somehow they cleared land and made habitations against wind and weather. Since the amount of food that colonists could bring with them was limited, they had to learn to plant the crops that would mature quickly. They brought seeds of grains and vegetables that they had known at home. Wheat was the most important food grain, but it took several months to grow and ripen. Because the loamy soils of the coastal region were not the best for wheat, the settlers in both Virginia and New England soon learned to adopt Indian methods of farming and to depend on corn as the staple grain.

The Indians had no plows and planted corn by digging a hole with a sharp stick, a deer antler, or an improvised wooden hoe. Into the hole they dropped four grains of corn, separated so they did not touch. They arranged the hills of corn four feet apart in straight lines. After the corn was up and about a foot high, they planted beans between

40

Captain John Smith captured by Indians. "They tyed him to a tree and as many as could stand about him prepared to shoot him." *From the Folger Library copy of John Smith,* Generall Historie of Virginia *(1624).*

the corn hills and allowed the bean vines to climb the cornstalks. This was a labor-saving device, making it unnecessary to find poles for the bean vines. The same field produced a crop of corn and a crop of beans, sometimes with a few pumpkins interspersed. The Virginia Indians used no fertilizer of any kind, observers reported. But in New England, where great schools of fish ran up the rivers in corn-planting time, the Indians caught fish and planted one under each hill of corn, a custom that the white settlers followed whenever they had sufficient fish.

To find enough cleared land for crops was one of the colonists' most difficult problems. The labor of cutting down and removing trees in a heavily forested area is enormous, even with power tools, and the colonists in the early years

King Powhatan comands C: Smith to be slaine, his daughter Pokahontas beggs his life, his thankfullness and how he subiected 39 of their kings. reade ý history.

printed by Iames Reeve

Pocahontas saves Captain John Smith: "being ready with their clubs to beate out his braines, Pocahontas, the King's dearest daughter . . . got his head in her armes, and laid her owne upon his." *From the Folger Library copy of John Smith,* Generall Historie of Virginia *(1624).*

did not have even a horse or an ox to drag the trees away. Hence they again adopted the Indian method of killing trees by "girdling" them—that is, by cutting a ring around the tree and removing the bark so that the sap could not rise. In time, the dead trees fell; but until then, crops grew between them. The earliest settlers along the Atlantic seaboard found some treeless land where the Indians had grown their crops, and they appropriated these fields. But as more settlers arrived they had to clear additional land. Every able-bodied colonist in the early years had to learn how to wield a woodsman's ax. For the frontiersman, the ax was the one implement that he could not do without. He might use a sharp stick or a deer antler in lieu of a plow, but he had to have an ax to fell a tree, or even to girdle it.

For the colonist, the deep, dark forests of the New World were sinister and terrifying. No seventeenth-century settler ever wrote a poem on the beauty of the forests primeval. These woods stood in his way and were alive with savage Indians and dangerous beasts. When he went into the woods, the settler felt ill at ease. The Indian, who was at home there, might be lurking anywhere. The fear of Indian-infested forests helps to explain why the Jamestown settlers

Captain John Smith turns the tables and takes the King of Pamaunkee prisoner. *From the Folger Library copy of John Smith, Generall Historie of Virginia (1624).*

C.Smith taketh the King of Pamavnkee prisoner 1608

in the winter of 1609–10 nearly starved although the nearby woods teemed with deer and other game. No white man dared venture far beyond the palisades in that desperate winter, for the little colony was too weak to make any concerted campaign to clear the Indians from their territory. The fear of the Indians and the dark forests that hid them also help to explain why the settlers clung to the coast for a long time and settled on necks of land that could be defended.

Although colonists everywhere in the early days lived in fear of marauding Indians, the red men were not invariably hostile. Indeed, the Jamestown settlers could not have survived if they had been unable to barter with the Indians for foodstuffs. For a number of years, John Rolfe's marriage to Pocahontas ensured peace with her father Powhatan, who was overlord of the Indians in that region. The Pilgrims who landed at Plymouth in December, 1620, owed much to the help of friendly Indians. Samoset and Squanto, two Indians who had had earlier contacts with English explorers, offered their services to the Pilgrims and helped them establish friendly relations with a neighboring tribe of Wampanoags whose chief was Massasoit. Thanks particularly to Squanto, who had been carried to England and returned, the Pilgrims lived in peace with their Indian neighbors, who taught them how to adapt to the new country. The Indians showed the white men how to plant crops, how to hunt and fish in the woods and streams, and where to find the best beaver and otter.

The early writers on America who emphasized the fruitfulness of the country and the abundance of all good things were not far wrong, for many edible plants, berries, and fruits were available for the picking; the fields and woods teemed with game; the streams were plentifully stocked with all manner of fish; and on the beaches and in the adjacent shallow salt water were clams and oysters in untold quantities. One would think that only a blind or an

Captain Argal, who came to Virginia after Smith left, in parley with Indians. Note trading for foodstuffs in background. *From the Folger Library copy of Theodor de Bry,* America, *Part X (1619).*

incredibly improvident person would have to go hungry. Yet at times the newcomers nearly perished, as at Jamestown during the "starving time." Not only did fear of Indians keep them from hunting, but ignorance of methods of catching fish and lack of nets and other equipment prevented them from utilizing the abundance of food surrounding them.

Hunger, however, is a great stimulus to ingenuity, and after their first unhappy experiences, the colonists in Virginia and New England learned to kill game and to catch fish. Indeed, by 1613, a minister, the Reverend Alexander Whitaker, wrote a little book entitled *Good News from Virginia* that described the quantities of fruits, game, and fish ready for man's sustenance. The ducks, geese, swans, and pigeons were numberless, though he added, "we want

45

the means to take them." Incredible quantities of fish, Whitaker declared, filled the rivers.

The sea fish come into our rivers in March and continue until the end of September; great schools of herrings come in first; shads of a great bigness and rockfish follow them. Trouts, bass, flounders, and other dainty fish come in before the other be gone; then come multitudes of great sturgeons, whereof we catch many and should do more but that we want good nets answerable to the breadth and depth of our rivers; besides our channels are so foul in the bottom with great logs and trees that we often break our nets upon them. I cannot reckon nor give proper names to the divers kinds of fresh fish in our rivers. I have caught with mine angle pike, carp, eel, perches of six several kinds, crayfish, and the torope [terrapin] or little turtle, besides many smaller kinds.

The worthy minister encouraged emigrants to set out from England with singing hearts, for they would be coming to a land of plenty. "Wherefore, since God hath filled the elements of earth, air, and water with his creatures, good for our food and nourishment," he wrote assuringly, "let not the fear of starving hereafter or of any great want dishearten your valiant minds from coming to a place of so great plenty." He added that they ought to bring along equipment for taking all the natural food available.

New England offered natural supplies of food in equal abundance. The Reverend Francis Higginson, who landed at Salem, Massachusetts, in April, 1629, wrote *New England's Plantation* (1630), in which he grew lyrical about New England and all its products. "A sup of New England's air," the minister declared, "is better than a whole draft of old England's ale." The fowls of the air, he asserted, were numerous and good for food. Partridges were as big as English hens, and turkeys, "often killed in the woods, far greater than our English turkeys and exceeding fat, sweet, and fleshy; here they have had abundance of feeding all the year long, as strawberries in summer (all places are full of them) and all manner of berries and fruits." The pigeons, geese, duck, and other game birds were so plentiful that a "great part of the winter planters have eaten nothing but roast meat of divers fowls which they have killed." Higginson also emphasized the ease of procuring ample supplies of good wood for fuel, something not readily available to a poor man in England. In short, he made New England sound like Paradise. Unhappily, poor Mr. Higginson died of tuberculosis, despite the wholesomeness of New England's air, the year after he landed.

Very early in America's history, hunting and fishing became a way of life. In fact, until the country became a nation of city-dwellers in the twentieth century, nearly every boy, even those who lived in cities, looked upon hunting and fishing as part of his birthright. In the period of

Pocahontas was the nickname, meaning "playful one," of Matoaka, daughter of Powhatan, chief of the tribe of that name and overlord of Virginia. She married Master John Rolfe, "an honest Gentleman," in 1613 and went to England where she was known as "the Lady Rebecca." Simon van de Passe engraving after a portrait by an unknown artist. *From the Folger Library copy of John Smith, Generall Historie of Virginia (1624).*

Friendly Indians taught the early settlers how to fish and to cook in the wilderness. *From the Folger Library copy of Theodor de Bry, America, Part I (1590).*

colonization the game of the woods and fields and the fish of the streams and sea were essential to life, and men and boys looked upon their guns, their snares and traps, their seines and nets and fishing lines, as necessary equipment for survival. They matched their wits against the cunning of wild animals and learned to be expert woodsmen. As soon as they lost their fear of the Indians and their terror of the dark woods, they began to regard hunting and fishing not only as a necessary means of procuring food but as a pleasurable sport as well.

The game birds that most astonished the early settlers were the wild pigeons, "passenger pigeons," as they came to be called, which were so numerous that they darkened the skies in flight and broke down trees by the sheer weight of their numbers. At night, these birds were easily confused by torchlights and were then slaughtered on their roosts with clubs. Indeed, the ease with which they were killed and the demand for pigeons as food brought about their complete annihilation in the nineteenth century.

Forests, which in many parts of the Atlantic seaboard extended almost to the edge of the sea, seemed not only mysterious and ominous to the first settlers but also hindered travel. Only occasional dim trails made by the Indians or by herds of deer wound through the dense growth of trees, underbrush, brambles, and vines. Briers caught on a traveler's clothes and tore his garments to shreds. Leather jackets and leather breeches were needed if one expected to penetrate the deep woods, either as a hunter or a traveler. Finding one's way through the woods was a hazardous undertaking, for there were few landmarks and the denseness of the growth frequently obscured the sun or the stars. Since seventeenth-century settlers had no pocket compasses to guide them, they risked getting lost. It is small wonder that they were awed by the great forests that surrounded

Indians taught the colonists to match their wits against the cunning of wild animals. *From the Folger Library copy of Theodor de Bry, America, Part II (1591).*

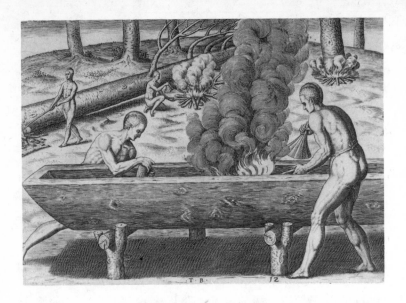

"Their Boats are but one great tree, which is but burnt in the forme of a trough with . . . fire, till it be as they would have it." Note tree girdled with fire in background. *From the Folger Library copy of Theodor de Bry,* America, *Part I (1590).*

In the absence of sawhorses such as they had known at home, the colonists dug sawpits to make their planks. *From the Folger Library copy of Jacob Cats,* Alle de Wercken *(1657–59).*

them and that they stayed as close as possible to waterways that offered convenient and easy means of transportation.

Fortunately, the Atlantic coast is laced with many fine rivers. Instead of being a barrier, the rivers were a godsend to the settlers who could use them for transport. For untold centuries the Indians had plied the inland waters in canoes, and the newcomers soon learned to make and use such craft. In the South, canoes were made by hollowing out tree trunks. These dugouts, or pirogues, drew little water and could be paddled or poled up streams too small for any other vessel. In the North, where large birch trees were to be found, Indians made canoes from strips of bark. These birchbark canoes were more fragile than dugouts, but they had the advantage of lightness and could be carried around rapids or overland to the next stream if need be. The white man quickly adopted the Indian canoe and made good use of it.

Canoes, however, were not adequate for moving heavy freight and for the carriage of farm products. For such use the settlers built heavier boats that could be rowed by several men, or small sloops that utilized a sail. In the early days when not a road existed in all of North America, some variety of floating craft was essential. Access to navigable water was a necessary consideration in choosing a spot for settlement.

The firstcomers were astonished by the great rivers that they found and were eager to claim land with river frontage. Most of the rivers along the Atlantic seaboard were deep enough to carry ocean-going ships for some distance into the interior. For many years, the "fall line"—the line where rocks and rapids blocked the passage of sailing ships —marked the limits of the white man's settlements. If he moved beyond that point, he had difficulty transporting his produce.

The early settlers had no market towns where they might

Riding a shingle-horse. The rough-cut shingle was held in the vise by one foot while the edges were trimmed with the draw knife. *Courtesy, Colonial Williamsburg, Williamsburg, Va. Photograph by John Crane.*

sell the products of their farms and no sources of supply for the goods they needed nearer than London or Bristol. Planters along the great rivers of tidewater Virginia and Maryland had their private docks where ocean-going ships could tie up and load. New England, also, had fine harbors where ships could anchor in safety. Most planters had "factors" serving as their agents in England to whom they shipped their produce and sent orders for the goods they needed. Some ship captains were traders in their own right who bought furs and other American products and sold powder and shot, foodstuffs, and articles of clothing to the colonists. It is hard for a modern American accustomed to all the goods available in a supermarket to imagine life without any market nearer than three thousand miles and with only a slow sailing ship as a means of delivery. A settler had to bring the essentials and thereafter have patience if he required anything further. A man might send an order to London for a coat and be pleased if he received it within a year.

A good site on a navigable stream, a place that could be defended against the Indians, and the promise of fertile soil once the trees were cleared—these were considerations in selecting a place for a settlement. Once having chosen a site, the settlers had to erect houses. Romantic writers have frequently talked about the log cabins built by the first immigrants. Actually, they built no log cabins, which were unknown in the England they had left. Log structures, however, were common in Sweden and Germany, and after Swedish and German settlers arrived and showed others how easy it was to notch logs and build them up pig-pen fashion, frontiersmen adopted this form of construction.

The early immigrants to Virginia, Maryland, New England, and other parts of the Atlantic seaboard built their first habitations out of wattles and mud, sticks and boughs plastered over with clay. A crude chimney was made of sticks with an inner lining of clay. A roof could be thatched with grass or pine boughs. Huts of this simple type, common in England, were easy to build with the material at hand. But as soon as settlers could afford the time and labor they cut tree trunks into convenient lengths and split off clapboards for more permanent houses. The implements required were simple; a blunt iron wedge called a froe and a wooden maul sufficed. Shingles or "shakes" were split in the same fashion from shorter lengths of a tree trunk. Planks they made by placing a log over a saw pit with one man above and one below in the pit to pull the handsaw.

The Prentis House, built in 1733 at Hadley, Mass., is a good example of the familiar saltbox style of many of the early homes. Typical of the English countryside of the time, the design seems to have developed from a shed or lean-to built onto an original structure. *Courtesy, Shelburne Museum, Inc., Shelburne, Vt. Photograph by Einars J. Mengis.*

With axes and adzes they hewed timbers square for uprights, corner posts, and sills. An infinite amount of labor went into the preparation of material for a house. The labor of setting the heavy timbers of the house frame in place was a cooperative effort among neighbors. "House-raisings" soon became festive occasions, with the owner of the house supplying food and drink for those who came to help.

Shelter against the weather and protection against enemies were the first essentials in each colony established in the New World. Over and over again, new settlers re-enacted the procedures of the earliest colonists. But no colonists were so inexperienced and ill-prepared as those who first landed at Jamestown, and the later settlers profited by the lessons their predecessors had learned the hard way. Promoters in London eventually learned that colonies sent out had to be properly equipped if they were to prosper. By the time of the beginning of the settlement of Pennsylvania in the period after 1681, emigrants had learned something about the climate and conditions of life in the wilderness world across the seas. They came better prepared and they suffered fewer hardships. Even so, a new life in the forests of America required courage, ingenuity, and a great capacity for hard work—qualities that were to characterize Americans henceforth.

3

Work and Play on the Farm, North and South

Until the beginning of this century, the United States was predominantly rural in its background. Most of the population had a knowledge of country life. For the first two hundred years after the settlement of North America, the majority of the people lived either on farms or in towns small enough to have intimate contact with the country. Every country boy and nearly every town boy knew what it meant to drive cows to the pasture, to milk a cow, and to take care of horses and pigs. Even in the mid-nineteenth century, pigs ran loose in the streets of New York City and served as scavengers. It was a point of pride for house-holders in towns to keep a milk cow. Many towns permitted the keeping of pigs and of course poultry. Nearly every house had a vegetable garden. The day of the super-market was still far in the distance and all citizens, old and young, knew something about the sources of the food they consumed.

A farming scene in the Old World typical, except for the castle ruin, of those reproduced by colonists in the New. *From the Folger Library copy of Diderot and D'Alembert,* Encyclopédie. Recueil des Planches *(1751–65).*

In the days of the early settlements, products of the land were essential to survival, and farming provided the means of subsistence in every section of the country. In the southern colonies, farms, particularly larger farms, were generally called "plantations" and their owners were known as planters. In the North, the term "farm" was more generally used. It could be of any size, as a ranch today in Southern California may consist of hundreds of acres or may be a small lot containing rabbit hutches or chicken coops.

At first the labor on the farms was supplied by the owner and his family. Gradually, laborers for hire became available and the amount of land that could be worked increased. In 1619 the first Negro servants were landed in Virginia, the forerunners of African slaves who would transform labor conditions on the larger plantations in the South and on a few in the North, for example, in New Jersey and Rhode Island. But even in the southern colonies

57

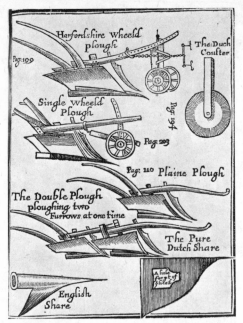

The first plows in colonial America showed little improvement over those used in the Middle Ages. *From the Folger Library copy of Walter Blith,* The English Improver Improved *(1652).*

the majority of the farmers owned few or no slaves and had to depend upon the labor of themselves and their families. In both North and South in the colonial period a great deal of labor was supplied by white bond servants—men, women, and children—who paid for their passage across the Atlantic by signing an indenture or contract to work for a definite period, usually ranging from four to seven years. At the expiration of their indentured period, they received a suit of clothes, a small amount of money and equipment, and departed to establish themselves as best they could as free men. From the position of indentured servant some became substantial citizens and a few rose to positions of prominence.

With African slaves, the situation was very different. They were slaves for life, and their children continued in the state of slavery. A few were freed by their owners; a few others managed by hard work to make enough to buy their own freedom. But by the end of the seventeenth century African slavery was thoroughly established. Northern shipowners and slave traders made immense profits from importing slaves from the West Coast of Africa, and the wealthier planters in the southern colonies discovered that they could utilize untrained Africans to do the heaviest work required in the fields and forests. For the next century and a half slavery would be the curse of American life.

But since only the well-to-do could afford to buy and keep slaves, most colonial Americans continued to work their own farms and supplement their own efforts with such labor as they could hire from time to time. An age like ours, accustomed to power tools and motorized equipment, can hardly conceive of the enormous human effort required

Like most farm equipment of the period, plows were made of wood. This so-called "Palatine" plow was used in the Mohawk Valley, New York, around 1750. *Courtesy, The Farmers' Museum, New York State Historical Association, Cooperstown, N.Y.*

to perform the ordinary work about a farm. The only power other than that of human brawn was supplied by a horse, mule, or ox. The first plows in colonial America showed little improvement over those used in the Middle Ages. Like most farm equipment of the period, plows were made of wood, the iron plowshare being the only metal in the whole implement. Even the teeth of harrows, needed to break the clods and smooth the plowed fields, were made of spikes of oak or hickory, wedged into a wooden frame. A heavy stone weight on top of the frame—and sometimes the weight of the boy driving the ox—gave the harrow sufficient pressure to crush the clods. Hay rakes and forks were also made of wood. The only vehicle on most farms was a two-wheeled cart. In many instances, wooden sledges dragged by two oxen sufficed for such hauling as might be required.

The symbolic importance of the plow in colonial farm life is shown by this wrought-iron weather vane, found in Maine. It is now at Old Sturbridge Village, Mass. *Courtesy, Old Sturbridge Village News Bureau, Sturbridge, Mass.*

Nobody in the colonial period ever heard of an eight-hour day. The workday on the farm was from sun to sun, sunup until sundown. Indeed, it was often longer than this, for livestock had to be fed and cows milked by lantern light in winter; even in the summer the farmer and his family were usually up and about their work long before sunrise. A farm permits no excuses. Horses and cattle must be fed and watered with clocklike regularity. Crops must be tended in accordance with weather conditions. When hay is lying dry upon the ground it must be raked and stacked before the rains come, even if the farmer and his family have to work until late at night. Ripe grain and ripe fruit will not wait upon the farmer's convenience. It must be reaped or gathered. The housewife must preserve or dry the fruits and vegetables when they are ready. On every farm the summer was a time of intense activity and endless labor.

But it was not mere drudgery. Farmers found satisfaction in their work, in watching the eternal re-creation of life each season, though not many ever stopped to put into words the reasons for their satisfaction. They enjoyed talk with the family and with neighbors about their growing crops—a constant subject of fascinating conversation to them. And they watched over their livestock and their poultry with abiding interest. Each horse, cow, sheep, or goat usually bore a name, sometimes a name that signified its appearance or some trait of disposition, and if farmers could not converse with their animals, at least they could talk to them by name. It was impossible to be lonely surrounded by so many breathing creatures with personalities worth observing. A part of the talk about the fireside in the evening would be about how Old Brindle or some other animal had behaved that day.

Since the weather, even in summer, was not invariably fair, there were days when it was too wet and rainy for much work out of doors. Such days were times for relaxa-

All tools were made of wood, and the only vehicle was a two-wheeled cart. *Courtesy, The Farmers' Museum, New York State Historical Association, Cooperstown, N.Y.*

tion and fun. Farm boys who did not mind the rain might go fishing or hunting in the woods. The period just after a rain was a good time to go "gigging" for turtles. With a barbed lance point fixed to the end of a stick a boy could probe the likely spots in the muddy streams until he pierced the shell of a turtle. The barb prevented the lance from pulling out and it was easy to drag the turtle to the surface. In the South turtle soup and turtle meat were regarded as delicacies from an early time, though terrapin was so common in Maryland that planters were warned against feeding their slaves exclusively on this diet. Today terrapin is one of the most expensive dishes in any restaurant.

Sports on rainy days were simple and sometimes crude. Boys frequently organized rat killings, which provided a certain amount of excitement. A group armed with clubs gathered around a pile of corn in the corncrib and slowly pitched the ears into a new pile. As the old pile dwindled, the rats harboring there ran out, to be clubbed to death on the crib floor. The boy with the largest number of rats to his credit was proclaimed champion rat killer. Sometimes wrestling matches would take place in the barns or corncribs. Sometimes boys and men would be content to sit around telling tales—ancient folk tales that had come down the centuries by word of mouth, or stories of recent adventures in the woods, or tales of ghosts or Indians, or of strange and wonderful happenings that defied explanation. Out of such story-telling sessions came the "tall tale" or exaggerated yarn told for comic effect. A farmer might

Many settlers had learned the care and management of livestock from English manuals such as *Markham's Maister:peece*, "touching the curing of all diseases in horses," published in 1636. *From the Folger Library copy.*

boast, for example, of the richness of his land. His watermelon vines grew so fast that they dragged the young melons along the ground at such a pace that they wore out before they had time to ripen. Such stories were legion. A rainy day in the summer was a time for fun if one had ingenuity and imagination—qualities that life in the New World stimulated.

Except in the South, the principal crops grown on the farms were foodstuffs. Indian corn or maize was a staple grain in every colony, though by the end of the seventeenth century wheat was common. Wheat was a particularly important crop in Pennsylvania and the colonies to the north. By the eighteenth century, when the upland regions of the Carolinas, Virginia, and Maryland were cleared and occupied, the production of wheat and other small grains—oats, rye, and barley—increased enormously.

Harvesting of these grains, which usually occurred in June or July, was hard work in the days before reaping machines. The usual implement was a small curved blade, a sickle, which had changed little in design since the days when Ruth gleaned the fields of Boaz, as the Old Testament reports. A scythe was a larger blade at the end of a handle which gave a longer reach and allowed the reaper to cut a wider swath. Picking up the stalks was more difficult after the sweeping stroke of the scythe, which scattered the cut stalks. Later a "cradle" was added to the scythe, which held the stalks in regular order until they could be gathered into a "hand" for bundling. The reaper usually had a man following him to tie the bundles and stack them into shocks. When the bundles were thoroughly dry they were taken to a threshing floor where men beat out the grain with long sticks called flails. The grain had to be winnowed clean on a windy day by pouring it from a height that permitted the wind to blow the chaff away. Although reaping and threshing were laborious tasks, they were usually the occasions for cooperative efforts by neigh-

64

Before the days of artificial fibers, men depended upon sheep for wool and pigs for bristles as well as bacon. *From the Folger Library copy of Jacob Cats,* Alle de Wercken *(1657–59).*

bors who gathered to help one another. The wives cooked special dinners for the reapers and threshers and provided vast stacks of pies and other good things to give this season of intense work the air of a festive occasion.

Indian corn matured much later than the small grains. But by late autumn, after a frost or two, the ears hung heavy and brown on the dry stalks. They were then pulled and taken to the corncribs where they were stored in the husks. Later in the season, when the more pressing work was over, corn shuckings would take place in the evenings. Cider or persimmon beer and cakes and cookies would be provided, and everybody would turn out to help shuck corn and enjoy a frolic.

A moonlight night in late November was a favorite time. A great pile of unshucked corn would be stacked on the ground at some convenient place and a bonfire would be lighted at a safe distance. Then the huskers would set to work. Most of the corn was yellow or white but an occasional red ear would turn up, a sign of good luck to the shucker who found it. Boys and girls particularly liked corn shuckings, which gave them a chance to have a party— and perhaps evade the curious eyes of their elders as they sought the shadows out of sight of the bonfires.

Indian corn provided the principal food for hogs and horses. Occasionally farmers fed corn meal to their milk cows. Since hogs flourished on corn, the production of pork products in corn-growing regions became an important industry and pork products early became a valuable export.

Cold weather in early winter was the favorite time for hog killing, an event that became an occasion for cooperation and jollity, especially with small farmers who had no hired help. The hog was hit on the head with an ax to stun it, and its throat was cut. Some people were careful to catch the blood for blood puddings. The hog was then hoisted up and dipped into a great kettle of scalding water. If a kettle was lacking, water might be heated in a cask with red-hot rocks. Scalding was necessary to loosen the bristles, which had to be scraped off. The animal was then hung head down from the crotch of a tree and disemboweled. Everything was saved. The small intestines, emptied and scraped clean, could be used for stuffing sausage, or they could be eaten as "chitterlings." Not everybody regarded chitterlings as an edible delicacy, but they were popular in some quarters. After the hog was cut up, the fat portions were tried into lard, some lean meat was ground into sausage or saved to be eaten fresh, and the rest— shoulders, hams, and bacon flanks—were salted and cured.

On rainy days "tall tales" were told around a kitchen hearth like this. Note clay pipes, and the dried herbs hanging from a rafter. *Courtesy, Old Sturbridge Village News Bureau, Sturbridge, Mass.*

Salt pork would keep under almost any conditions if enough salt was used; it became a staple of diet on long sea voyages and an important article in colonial American commerce.

Beef might be salted in much the same way, or pickled in brine to become corned beef. Since it too would keep, corned beef also became an important article for sale to ship captains and for export abroad.

The German farmers in the back country of Pennsylvania, a particularly provident and thrifty group, produced vast quantities of foodstuffs of all sorts: grains, meat products, fruits, dried vegetables, and dried fruits. They even dried young Indian corn in such a way that it could be soaked and cooked into dishes that tasted almost like fresh corn. These food products they hauled to Philadelphia in stout covered wagons that could operate over the rough wagon roads of the day. By the mid-eighteenth century, Philadelphia was a great port filled with ships that plied the seven seas, and there the German farmers found a ready market for the products of their farms. These farmers helped to bring prosperity to the colony of Pennsylvania and to the city of Philadelphia. They also taught other people much about the good things that the earth could produce.

Because of differences in soil, climatic conditions, and the background of the people themselves, farming methods varied from region to region, but the life of farmers who actually worked the land was much the same everywhere.

The herbs that hung in colonial kitchens provided not only seasoning but the family medicine chest. This herb garden of "urban" Williamsburg is probably more formal than most, with its diamond parterre pattern and clipped hedges. *Courtesy, Colonial Williamsburg, Williamsburg, Va.*

An unceasing routine kept men, women, and children busy, but life was not grim. Work was interspersed with simple pleasures. Food was abundant and no man lived in danger of starvation, as many had in seventeenth- and eighteenth-century Europe. To the sturdy American farmer, wherever he lived, the future seemed bright. Land was easy to come by, and if he did not like the particular spot he had chosen, he could go somewhere else. By the labor of his own hands he could hope to attain at least moderate comforts and some degree of prosperity. He had independence and freedom and felt that he was master of his own fate. Some things he found to grumble about, to be sure, for grumbling is part of the nature of man, but the small farmer in all of the colonies had the essentials that made for an independent and good life.

During the eighteenth century, the great valley of Virginia was settled with German and Scottish immigrants who had landed in Philadelphia and had gradually filtered into the inland valleys in search of cheap land. Some Scottish immigrants came by way of Charleston, South Carolina. They pushed on into the hill country of South and North Carolina, and finding the best land in those regions already occupied, they continued into the high lands of Virginia and occupied the fertile valleys they discovered there. To this day Scottish names outnumber most others in many valley communities from the Carolinas to Maryland; Germans also settled in these localities and made substantial contributions to the development of the country. They were better farmers than the Scots and proved useful by setting an example and showing the way for improved forms of agriculture. Immigrant Scots soon learned from them that there were better foods than oatmeal, and that other grains besides oats—which Dr. Samuel Johnson defined as food for men in Scotland and for horses in England—would grow in the rich soil of the valley of the Shenandoah and its tributaries.

Scots who settled in the hill country of South Carolina discovered that wild pea vines, which grew in abundance, provided a highly nutritious food for cattle. They had been accustomed to raising cattle on the Scottish moors, but they had never known a country before with such quantities of foodstuff for their animals, available without the slightest exertion on their part. So cattle raising quickly became an important industry in this region. To market their cattle, they had to drive them over rough trails to Charleston. As in California before the American occupation, some cattle were slaughtered merely for their hides and tallow, needed for leather and candles. The Scottish herdsmen of upper South Carolina during the colonial period were a rough and unruly lot, the first American cowboys. The center of their activities was a settlement called Cowpens, the scene of a famous battle during the Revolution.

In the coastal region of Virginia and Maryland tobacco was the main crop, as it had been from the beginning. This single crop had brought riches to planters whose fine houses could be seen along the tidal rivers. Each house had its own dock where ships from the Old World called to take on tobacco and to unload the luxuries that tobacco made possible.

To John Rolfe, who had married the Indian girl Pocahontas, these colonies owed the first commercial development of tobacco as a money crop. The earliest explorers had observed the Indians smoking native tobacco, a pungent and biting variety, which Englishmen did not relish. But John Rolfe by some means procured seed of tobacco grown in the Caribbean islands and in South America. This species, sweeter and better suited to the taste of Englishmen, proved highly successful, and very soon after 1614, when Rolfe made his first shipment of the improved tobacco to London, everybody in Jamestown was diligently planting tobacco. The price on the London market was so high that some sailors deserted their ships and hid on shore in

70

Harvesting wheat was hard work in the days before reaping machines. Here the farmer's wife gathers the stalks into a "hand" for bundling. *From the Folger Library copy of Jacob Cats,* Alle de Wercken *(1657–59).*

order to plant a crop of tobacco in the rich soil that was available once the danger of Indian attacks was past. So eager were settlers to grow the profitable weed that they planted it in the very streets of Jamestown.

In the early days of settlement, tobacco sold for sixpence per pound at the dock in Virginia, a price roughly equivalent to $1.20 in modern American currency. It is small wonder that everybody wanted to grow the weed. The eagerness to plant tobacco inevitably resulted in its overproduction. By 1650 the price had dropped to threepence a pound, and by 1662 it was bringing only twopence a pound. In that year a group of large planters and merchants petitioned the King to forbid the planting of tobacco

71

for one year so that demand could catch up with production, but this plea was rejected. From time to time during the following years, however, efforts were made to curb production, and in some instances "night riders" went about the country cutting up the growing crops in order to restrict the quantity produced and thus raise the price.

Although the price of tobacco fluctuated during the colonial period, it remained the crop that produced the most certain income for small farmers as well as for large planters. In Virginia and Maryland, debts were paid in tobacco, and even the ministers received so many pounds of tobacco as their salaries, for currency was scarce and the normal medium of exchange was tobacco. The large planters with docks on deep water where ocean-going vessels could tie up bought tobacco from small farmers and included it with their own shipments. They also ordered supplies from their agents in England for their less prosperous neighbors and took payment in tobacco.

For shipment, tobacco was usually packed in great hogsheads weighing from 375 to 475 pounds each. These could be rolled along the ground to the docks. In places far from convenient water transportation, farmers cleared a path known as a rolling road through the woods and across fields so that the hogsheads could be rolled to a point where they could be loaded on barges or ships. Tobacco was at times loaded on ships in bulk without being packed in casks, but this was regarded as a wasteful and undesirable method of shipping.

The arrival of tobacco ships in the Virginia and Maryland rivers was an occasion for excitement. Ship captains came ashore to enjoy the hospitality of the planters and to regale them with news and stories of the lands across the seas. Sailors and shipboys also came ashore to spin yarns of life at sea: of pirates barely missed, of sea serpents large enough to sink a ship, of whales, and of sharks waiting for a man to fall overboard, of ships becalmed or tossed by tempests—all stories designed to leave colonial youths wide-eyed with wonder. To old and young of every station, the arrival of the tobacco fleets brought a thrill of pleasure and broke the monotony of provincial life.

In the tobacco colonies this weed dominated the thought and actions of everyone. Every man's livelihood depended upon this one crop, and the state of its cultivation and the price it brought were matters for constant talk and speculation. Although some foodstuffs were grown on plantations and farms, the predominant crop was tobacco, for it was the one article that could be used in place of money.

From the time in the spring when the seeds were sown in beds until the leaves were cured in the late summer, men watched over their tobacco fields with anxious care. With hoes they removed grass and weeds. By hand they picked off caterpillars and other worms that threatened to riddle the broad green leaves. They also watched with anxiety the storm clouds of midsummer, for a hailstorm could ruin the crop in a matter of minutes. When at last the ripe leaves, just turning a pale yellow-green, were plucked, tied into "hands," and slowly dried on sticks suspended in the tobacco barns, the planters could breathe easier.

Tobacco-growing was hard on the land. Continuous planting exhausted the soil after about seven years, and fresh land had to be cleared and planted. That helps to explain why men in the tobacco colonies were greedy for large grants of land. They had to have ample tracts for new tobacco fields every seven years.

When the crop was gathered and cured, tobacco growers could take their ease. This was a time for musters of the militia, for horse races, and for other forms of jollification. Every able-bodied man was supposed to turn out for drill when the colonel of the militia, usually the most prominent planter in the county, called for a muster. But drilling was not the only occupation of muster day. There was much drinking of cider and beer, cardplaying, storytelling, and

73

In the tobacco colonies the "weed" dominated the thought and actions of everyone. *From the Huntington Library copy of* The Universal Magazine, *Nov., 1750.*

sometimes fighting to add to the excitement. Everybody also turned out for horse racing, and for other forms of sports less exalted, such as running after a greased pig or "gander pulling," in which men rode by and tried to pull off the well-greased head of a goose suspended from a bar. When a rider lost his balance and tumbled to the ground, the crowd held their sides with laughter. Our ancestors were not overly refined and they did not worry about such things as pain to the goose or danger to the rider.

Farther to the south other crops took the place of tobacco. In South Carolina rice was introduced in the late years of the seventeenth century. A sea captain named John Thurber brought some seed from Madagascar, and the East India Company sent a small bag of rice seed from

Tobacco "production line" on a large plantation. *From Jean Baptiste du Tertre*, Histoire Générale des Antilles *(1667), Vol. II, in the Arents Tobacco Collection, New York Public Library.*

India. By 1700 enough rice was being grown for export to England and the West Indies, and from then until late in the nineteenth century rice was one of the most important crops in South Carolina.

The cultivation of rice required flat land that could be flooded during the growing season and drained when the grain matured. The coastal lands of South Carolina and parts of North Carolina and Georgia were ideal for this purpose because of the many rivers from which fresh water could be channeled into the fields. An intricate system of canals and sluice gates controlled the flow of water. At intervals disaster struck the rice fields, as when a hurricane drove salt water over the fields or a spring freshet turned the rivers into uncontrollable torrents. With canal dykes ruined and sluice gates swept away, the rice planter had to start afresh and devote a season to engineering before another crop could be planted.

75

Rice was reaped like any other grain, but its preparation for use as a food required two processes. First the grains had to be threshed from the straw and then pounded in a pestle until the brown husks were separated from the white grains that we know. It was then ready for cooking. Rice quickly became a staple of diet. To this day South Carolinians probably eat more rice than other Americans because their ancestors established a pattern of using rice in many ways.

South Carolina had another important crop in indigo, a plant from which a blue dye was extracted. Before the invention of chemical dyes, most dyes came from vegetables; and the blue for soldiers' and sailors' garb came from indigo. The cultivation of this tropical plant was demonstrated by a talented young woman named Eliza Lucas, daughter of a British naval officer who had been stationed in the West Indies before moving to South Carolina. Eliza Lucas, who had seen indigo growing on the island of An-

The production of indigo required hard labor and increased the demand for African slaves. *From the Folger Library copy of Pierre Pomet,* Compleat History of Druggs *(1737).*

tigua, successfully cultivated it on her father's plantation near Charleston about 1741. Within five years the colony was producing enough indigo dye to make it an important export. Processing the plants to extract the dye was a laborious and messy process, but the profits were high and indigo continued to be an important crop throughout the colonial period.

Processing indigo required no great skill, but workers had to endure hard labor and to tolerate the slimy vats where the plants soaked. African slaves proved useful in this work, and the production of indigo, like the cultivation of rice, increased the demand for slaves and stimulated the trade with the slave merchants of New England.

South Carolina planters lived on their plantations along the network of rivers during the winter, but when summer came with its swarms of mosquitoes, the planters moved to Charleston, where they occupied their town houses. These were built with wide verandas so placed that they took advantage of the ocean breezes. Life in Charleston during "the season" was festive and gay for the well-to-do planters and merchants. Dances, musicales, and an endless round of dinners and social gatherings entertained old and young alike. When autumn came and the planters could return to their homes along the rivers, they could look forward to hunting wild turkey and deer and to fishing for bass in the black waters of the streams and lakes.

From an early time, Englishmen had hoped that their colonies could produce silk, which they had been forced to buy at high prices from foreign sources. Fashionable men and women wore silken garments, and a vast amount of money went out of England every year to pay for extravagant dress. King James I had urged Virginians to raise silkworms for the production of raw silk and had provided the colonists with a book by a Frenchman telling how this could be done. But the Virginians had not seen fit to follow this royal advice. Later, in South Carolina and

Fashionable attire such as this was made of silk, which England
hoped to produce in the colonies. The dream did not materialize—
until the eventual invention of nylon. *From the Folger Library copy
of Wenceslaus Hollar,* Ornatus Muliebris Anglicanus *(1640).*

Georgia, a few French and Swiss immigrants had experimented with silk culture and actually produced small quantities. Georgia was so hopeful of the silk industry that the first settlers were required to plant a certain number of mulberry trees, the leaves of which provided the food needed by silkworms. But the tedious labor required to raise silkworms and to wind the raw silk from their cocoons made silk production in the American colonies so unprofitable that the industry never flourished.

By the end of the colonial period, the whole Atlantic seaboard was dotted with prosperous farms and plantations, some small, some large, but all producing a variety of products that sustained the population and provided commodities for export to the markets of the Caribbean islands and to Europe. Upon these farms dwelt an increasing population of men and women whose way of life taught them self-reliance and a spirit of vigorous independence. One dark blot spoiled the picture of idyllic country life. That was the stain of slavery, which troubled many men, including Thomas Jefferson and others of his contemporaries.

4

Fishing, Shipbuilding, and
Products From the Forests

No man knows how long Europeans have fished in the waters off the coast of North America. Some scholars believe that fishermen from Brittany, Spain, Portugal, or England may have reached Newfoundland and the shores of what is now New England before Columbus made his first voyage to the Caribbean. If the first men to discover the cod fisheries of the North Atlantic are unknown to history, at least we can be certain that by the end of the sixteenth century the maritime nations of Europe were aware of the advantages of commercial fishing in those waters.

In 1583, Sir Humphrey Gilbert sailed into St. John's Harbor in Newfoundland and claimed that island for England, but he discovered that its shores were already teeming with fishermen from half a dozen countries. They were a rough and restless lot, who kept an uneasy peace among themselves without benefit of formal law of any nation.

Fishermen brought their catches ashore, erected wooden platforms, salted and dried their codfish, and occasionally quarreled and rioted.

The news of the vast quantities of fish in these northern waters convinced some Englishmen that fishing might be more profitable than the search for gold, which had proved a vain delusion for many years. Captain John Smith, for example, in *A Description of New England,* described the riches that he believed might be gained from the sea, and he cited the example of Dutch fishermen who had made "the sea the source of those silvered streams of all their virtue." Smith was one of the first to emphasize the staple products to be derived from the sea and forests of New

Sir Humphrey Gilbert who, in 1583, claimed Newfoundland for England. On the voyage home he and his ship were lost at sea after Gilbert, sitting calmly aft with a book in his hand, uttered his immortal line: "We are as near to Heaven by sea as by land!" *From the Folger Library copy of Henry Holland,* Herωologia Anglica *(1620).*

England. When King James heard that the Pilgrims who settled at Plymouth in 1620–21 proposed to make their way by fishing, he commented that it was a good trade, exercised by the Holy Apostles, and he wished them well.

New England settlers early discovered that the sea and the woods could provide a more bountiful livelihood than they could expect to wring from the land. Except for the river valleys and some flat areas near the coast, New England's soil was thin and less fertile than the lands farther south. Farmers along the coast added to their income by fishing, by trading with the Indians, by cutting ship timbers and making barrel staves from the oaks in their forests, and by building boats and small ships. New Englanders were often skilled craftsmen as well as farmers, and they were never dependent upon a single commodity as were the planters of Virginia and Maryland.

The combined occupations of farming, fishing, trading, and manufacturing kept the settlers of New England exceedingly busy, but this diversity of enterprise ensured their ultimate prosperity. As early as 1624 a ship carpenter at Plymouth built two shallops, which the men of Plymouth used in fishing and in trading with the Indians as far away as the Kennebec River in Maine. The colonists already had a surplus of corn to use in trade with the improvident Indians, who frequently exhausted their food supplies before the next crop matured. On one expedition to the Kennebec, Governor Edward Winslow of Plymouth traded for 700 pounds of beaver pelts and other furs. From this time forward, the fur trade ranked close behind fishing as a profitable enterprise. Beaver, mink, and marten skins were in great demand in England and brought good prices.

The fishing industry of New England outstripped in importance all other commercial activities in the first century of settlement. And of the fish taken, the codfish was by far the most valuable because it could be cured and dried with salt and then sold at a good price in southern Europe.

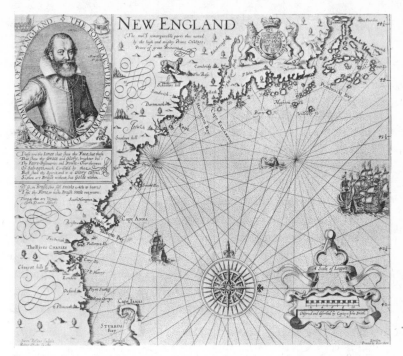

Captain John Smith's map of New England on which Prince Charles, son of James I, wrote the English names. Smith urged the pursuit of the "silvered streams" of fish instead of gold. *From the Church copy in the Huntington Library of John Smith,* A Description of New England *(1616).*

Protestant New England supplied much of the fish that Catholic Italy, Spain, and Portugal consumed on fish days.

Codfish were of various sorts. The most favored type, the "dun-fish," so called because of its color, was taken in the open sea in the winter months. A large fat fish, it could be cured and dried without losing its appetizing moist character.

Codfishing was work for men with stout hearts and strong muscles. During the spring and summer months, fishermen set out from Boston, Plymouth, Salem, Gloucester, Marblehead, and many other fishing ports along the New England coast with the Newfoundland Banks as their destination.

In those cold and misty seas they were not without company, for the fleets of many nations frequented the Banks in search of fish that flourished there in unnumbered millions. By the eighteenth century, the normal fishing craft bound for Newfoundland out of New England was a schooner with a crew of six or eight men and a couple of boys. Such a vessel usually made two or three round trips to the fishing grounds in the course of the spring and early summer.

Contrary to popular opinion, codfishing was done with hand lines and with nets. The fishermen carried along barrels of freshly caught mackerel pickled in brine, which they used for bait. The greedy cod was easy to take with a hook and, once in a school of the fish, the busy linesmen had little trouble in landing a cargo. But merely hauling the fish aboard was not the end of the labor. The fish were split, cleaned, and salted down aboard ship. A portion of

Seining, the method of fishing for mackerel in bays and inlets. *From the Folger Library copy of Jacob Cats,* Alle de Wercken *(1657–59).*

the crew, with the help of the boys, kept busy cleaning fish, a smelly and messy task. Entrails were tossed overboard for the gulls, but the heads were frequently retained for hog food. Cods' tongues, regarded as delicacies, were carefully preserved. Nobody had yet discovered that the livers were sources of vitamins; but liver oil was valued for treating leather, and one of the duties of the ship's boys was to save the livers.

Colonial fishing craft had no refrigeration, of course, but salt was a preservative that kept fish from spoiling. Those not intended for drying were kept in brine and regarded as "fresh" fish. Once the fishermen had taken an ample cargo, they pulled up anchor and sailed for their home ports. They still had a vast amount of labor ahead of them. The salted fish were unloaded, washed in salt water, and spread to dry on platforms called flakes. After the drying process had started, no water was allowed to touch them. Once dry, the "stockfish" were ready for export to the Mediterranean countries.

Not all codfishing was done over the Newfoundland Banks. Many fish were taken off the New England shores by men and boys who went out in rowboats and dories. Even in the chill autumn and early winter, these fishermen braved the open sea to take fish that abounded offshore. Many of the commonwealth's hardiest citizens spent their lives seeking the codfish that brought prosperity to the whole region. It is small wonder that the codfish became the official emblem of the state of Massachusetts.

But cod was not the only fish that had commercial value. Every spring and autumn great schools of mackerel entered the bays and sounds along the New England coast, where they were taken in nets. The mackerel were pickled in brine to be used as bait, or they were shipped to the West Indies, where they were in demand as food for slaves. Other fish, regarded as unfit for sale to the Mediterranean trade, found a market in the West Indies. Slave-masters

85

were not squeamish about the food they supplied their charges, and New England shippers were glad to find a ready sale for products that nobody else would use.

During the spring runs of herring and shad, New England streams were choked with fish, which could be dipped out with nets and loaded on carts. Large herring-type fish called alewives were so plentiful that they were taken by the wagonload and used for fertilizer. This was the fish that the Indians taught the Plymouth settlers to plant with their seed-corn. The shad, a type of herring, was used for food locally during the spring runs, and some were smoked and dried for future use.

Salmon were taken in weirs or traps in the rivers, but the art of canning salmon was yet in the future and New Englanders were too preoccupied with drying codfish and pickling mackerel to develop a market for smoked salmon.

Fishing was such an important occupation that not much is said in the colonial records about fishing for sport. But not everybody who took a fishing line in hand was a commercial fisherman, and men and boys then as now enjoyed pitting their cunning against trout and salmon.

Rivers and streams abounded with a greater variety of fish than now, for pollution had not poisoned them and dams had not stopped their annual spawning migrations upstream. Sturgeon, common in the rivers, were not much prized as a food fish, because they were "coarse" and no New Englander at this time thought of curing sturgeon roe into caviar.

Whaling, which became a profitable industry in New England in the eighteenth century, had an early beginning in port towns, which encouraged their citizens to watch for "drift whales"—whales that got too close to shore and were stranded in shallow water. Whales, common in North Atlantic waters, were frequently seen in Long Island Sound and occasionally in Boston and New York harbors. Plymouth in 1654 made a law that a whale cast up on any man's private land was the property of the landowner. Now-

A "drift whale," probably a right whale, and the windlasses used to bring it ashore. *From the Folger Library copy of Awnsham and Churchill,* A Collection of Voyages *(1704).*

adays a whale stranded on one's beach is a nuisance and a problem for the sanitation department. But in the seventeenth century, such a gift from the sea—if not too far gone in decomposition—was a find of great value, for the blubber would yield oil prized for lamps, and the bonelike strainers in the throat of the whale called "baleen" provided the "whalebone" used in stiffening women's garments.

The two whales most commonly found in the North Atlantic waters were right whales and sperm whales; both grew to enormous size, sometimes 55 or 60 feet in length. The right whales were the ones that most frequently drifted ashore; the sperm whales stayed farther out at sea but could be taken by boatmen armed with harpoons. They were especially prized because of the sperm oil found in their heads, an oil that made one of the best lubricants yet discovered. A secretion called ambergris, which whales ejected into the water, floated ashore and was found from time to time on the beaches. It was used as a base for perfumes and had a high monetary value.

Indians from time out of mind had sought whales offshore. *From the Folger Library copy of Theodor de Bry,* America, *Part IX (1602).*

Long Islanders took the lead in the earliest whale fishing, but the men of Plymouth and Nantucket were not far behind. The area from Long Island Sound to Nova Scotia teemed with both right and sperm whales, but, later in the eighteenth century, whaling voyages extended as far as the coasts of Brazil and West Africa. By the nineteenth century, whalers from Nantucket and New Bedford were going on voyages that took them around Cape Horn into the South Pacific.

Colonial whaling expeditions were of two sorts: in rowboats that put out from shore when a whale was sighted, and in small sailing ships with boats that could be lowered to pursue the whale. A boat crew consisted of four to six oarsmen and a harpoon man, who stood poised in the bow ready to drive his iron deep into the whale. His aim had to be as true as that of a bullfighter in order to hit a vital spot. Attached to the harpoon was a long line, coiled so that it could pay out without tangling or capsizing the boat, for the whale was likely to "sound" (dive) at great speed. Eventually, when the huge creature was exhausted and dying, it would be towed to shore; or, if the craft was equipped for "trying out" (melting) the blubber into oil, the whale would be drawn alongside the ship.

The pursuit of a whale was a dangerous but exciting adventure. Much depended upon the skill of the harpooner, who had to have a quick eye and unerring skill with his lance. Many of the best harpoon men were Indians who from time out of mind had sought whales offshore. The oarsmen also had to be skillful and alert, for it was their business to keep the boat out of range of the whale's flailing tail, which could smash a boat with a single blow. Usually whales were not belligerent and were intent only upon escaping, but occasionally a wounded whale would turn on a boat and crush it like an eggshell between its jaws. In a few recorded instances whales drove headlong into sailing ships with such force that they stove in the timbers and sank the vessels.

Once a dead whale lay alongside a whaling ship, crewmen stripped off its blubber in flakes with a hoe-like instrument and hoisted it aboard. In iron pots set on bricks to protect the decks from fire, the fat was melted into oil that could be drained into casks. The whalebone was salvaged and the remaining carcass was left to the sharks. The lean whale meat was not yet an item that New England fishermen could market. If whales were taken near enough to be towed to shore, trying out the oil could be accomplished more easily there than at sea. Some of the whale meat could also be salvaged for hog food.

Whale oil was valuable because whale-oil lamps gave a clearer light than tallow candles, and many householders wanted this improved form of illumination. The profits from whaling induced more and more seafarers to adopt this

Several versions of the whale-oil lamp. *Courtesy, Old Sturbridge Village News Bureau, Sturbridge, Mass.*

trade, and by the end of the colonial period, in towns like New Bedford and Nantucket, a large proportion of the population had some connection with whaling—either as active participants or as suppliers of equipment and dealers in oil. The method of dividing the profits of a whaling expedition was calculated to stimulate the interest and activity of each individual, because everyone received a specified portion of the profits. Even the lowliest ship's boy had a promised share and knew what his proportion of the profits would be. So enticing was whaling that by 1775 Nantucket alone had some one hundred fifty whaling vessels at sea. Although Nantucket was the main center of the industry, ports all along the North Atlantic coast sent out whalers. To encourage the industry, Connecticut excused whalers, as well as cod fishermen, from paying taxes.

Deep-sea fishermen and whalers sometimes made a profit from commodities that they did not talk about. Some of these men were not above taking on a cargo of goods from foreign vessels off the coast of Newfoundland or Nova Scotia and smuggling them into port without paying duty. During the colonial period, Great Britain attempted to see that all goods shipped to the colonies came from British markets in British vessels. Foreign goods were often cheaper. Many a fisherman came home to Boston or some other port with French or Spanish wines buried beneath his fish, or with fabrics and clothing from non-British sources. Colonials did not approve of the so-called navigation acts that curbed their trading with foreign countries, and they felt no compunction about smuggling when they could escape the port inspectors.

Besides the normal hazards of the sea, fishermen and whalers in the North Atlantic had other dangers to face during the wars that raged intermittently between the European powers in the late seventeenth and eighteenth centuries. Privateers—ships equipped with "letters of marque," which granted them the privilege of capturing vessels of belligerent nations—preyed upon the hapless fishermen, taking their cargoes when they needed supplies, seizing or destroying their vessels, and sometimes kidnapping crewmen. In addition to the danger from privateers, the sea lanes were harassed always with ordinary pirates, who were not interested in fish but might need to pillage a fishing vessel for supplies. The life of a fisherman or whaler did not suffer from monotony.

The fishing industry created a demand for boats and ships, which New England shipyards began to supply in the early years of settlement. The first vessel of any size was a 30-ton craft built at Mystic (now Medford, Mass.) for Governor John Winthrop of Massachusetts Bay Colony. It was launched on July 4, 1631, and christened *The Blessing of the Bay*. This event foreshadowed the development of a vast enterprise for Americans, for shipbuilding in the following two centuries became one of the country's most important industries.

As the ports along the Atlantic seaboard grew in size and as commerce increased, the demand for ocean-going craft became more pressing. Shipyards, great and small, sprang up in ports where enough skilled carpenters could be found. Sometimes the commanders of English warships and merchant vessels, wintering in American ports, hired out some craftsmen from their crews to work in local ship-yards. This practice often caused difficulties when the vessels were ready to sail, for many of these craftsmen preferred to stay ashore, and on sailing day they could not be found.

Ocean-going craft built in New England were often small shallops, flyboats, and ketches, but they were built to withstand rough weather and were capable of making long voyages. At the end of the seventeenth century most colonial-built vessels were under a hundred tons, and many were much smaller. Some 15- and 20-ton vessels made voyages to Newfoundland, the South Atlantic coast, the West Indies, and even crossed the Atlantic to Europe. The price for building vessels in New England averaged something like £4 per ton in the early years of the eighteenth century, or roughly $200 per ton in today's currency. A small trader could not afford and did not need a vessel of 100 tons' burden, but for the equivalent of $4,000 in our money he could have a 20-ton vessel useful in the coastal trade. In the early eighteenth century, William Byrd of Westover in Virginia complained about small craft from New England that sailed up the Virginia rivers and engaged in illegal barter with slaves, who were not averse to slipping a little of their master's tobacco into the shipmaster's hands in return for trinkets or a bit of gay cloth.

As shipbuilding increased during the eighteenth century, the industry required many forest products, not all of which New England could supply. North and South Carolina, where the rosin-rich longleaf pine flourished, produced large quantities of tar, rosin, and turpentine needed for

Without barrels commerce in colonial times would have come to a standstill. The cooper's trade was a key industry. *From the Folger Library copy of Diderot and D'Alembert,* Encyclopédie. Recueil des Planches *(1751–65).*

paint, not only for the colonial trade but for the English market as well. Such ships' stores derived from Southern forests are still important commodities in international trade.

One reason why Great Britain had been eager for colonies in North America was the necessity of finding a source of forest products that would free her from dependence upon the Baltic countries, then, as now, important producers of timber and related commodities. Great Britain had been improvident in the use of her own forests and lacked sufficient oaks to provide ship timbers and other lumber. So barren was Scotland of woods in the seventeenth century that someone remarked that Judas could have found salvation sooner than a tree on which to hang himself. The manufacture of iron and steel required charcoal, obtained from the burning of timber in kilns, and England needed

Molasses for New England's rum. A West Indies sugar mill engaged in the "triangular trade." *From the Huntington Library copy of Jean Baptiste du Tertre*, Histoire Générale des Antilles (*4 vols., Paris, (1667–71).*

charcoal. The mother country turned to the forests of America for all of these products.

Tall spruce and pine trees were required for masts of the ships of war that made Great Britain mistress of the seas. In the seventeenth and eighteenth centuries, officers of the Royal Navy went through American forests along the seaboard from Maine to the Carolinas marking especially fine trees with the broad arrow that indicated that the tree was reserved for the King's ships. Nobody could legally cut or harm such a tree; but if it was on private land, once it was cut down, the owner might collect its fair price from the King's officers. Many disputes arose over the cutting and pricing of such trees.

Ships were built with the dimensions and tonnage needed to transport masts to England. A ship of 400 tons and a crew of twenty-five men could carry forty-five or fifty masts across the Atlantic. Such masts were required to measure between twenty-four and thirty-six inches in diameter at the base, and to have a length in feet equal to the number of inches of the butt's diameter multiplied by three. Thus a mast twenty-four inches in diameter would measure seventy-two feet in length.

The colonies also carried on a considerable trade with Spain and Portugal in ships' spars, timbers, and masts. Since England was periodically at war with these nations, and did not look with favor upon trading with an enemy, she periodically forbade such shipments.

One of the most important forest products was the lowly barrel stave, which could be split from red or white oak and smoothed and shaped with a minimum of skill. Making barrel or pipe staves, as they were generally called (from the word "pipe" meaning a wine cask), provided employment for countless men and boys throughout the seventeenth and eighteenth centuries. Wooden barrels had many uses, and without them commerce would have come to a standstill. Ships had to have barrels to hold supplies

A cheese press of yellow poplar, with ash and walnut, at the Raleigh Tavern. *Courtesy, Colonial Williamsburg, Williamsburg, Va.*

of water and beer. Barrels were needed in the wine-making countries, for without barrels they could not store and ship their wines. Barrels were needed in the West Indies for the sugar and molasses trade. Indeed, practically all food-stuffs and many other products were stored and shipped in barrels. Because Sir Francis Drake, long before the American trade developed, burned Spanish ships bringing cargoes of well-cured barrel staves needed by the Spanish navy, the Spanish Armada had to go to sea with its water and wine stored in casks made of green timber that leaked and spoiled the precious supplies. This loss helps to account for England's victory in 1588. Thus the makings for barrels were extremely important, and colonial traders developed

Ingenious homemade candle lantern with top probably salvaged from a more professionally made pierced tin lantern. *Courtesy, Old Sturbridge Village News Bureau, Sturbridge, Mass.*

a profitable market for them in the West Indies and the "Wine Islands" of Madeira and the Canaries.

Many of the barrels made in New England played a part in the profitable "triangular trade" that developed in the eighteenth century. From molasses obtained in the West Indies, distillers in Boston, Newport, and other towns made rum which they shipped to the west coast of Africa. There they bartered their rum for Negro slaves whom they brought back and sold to sugar planters in the West Indies. Again loading molasses, they returned to New England and distilled more rum. This trade made immense profits for distillers, shippers, and slave traders.

New Englanders in particular found the manufacture of woodenware a profitable use of their spare time and a valuable source of income. During the long winter evenings, men and boys made numerous small objects ranging from churns and churn dashers to wooden spoons and trenchers, a sort of wooden plate commonly used at table. Colonial boys learned to whittle with a purpose and to make a profit from their whittling.

Besides timber, the forests of the Atlantic region provided another continuing source of income and profit for colonial Americans. The earliest settlers had recognized the value of beaver and other furs and had traded with the Indians for pelts. As the Atlantic settlements multiplied, the competition for furs became more acute, not only among English settlers, but also with the French in Canada. All along the coast from Maine to Georgia, traders combed the back country to find trappers, both white and Indian, from whom they could obtain furs and deerskins.

Rivalry over the fur trade helped to keep the English and French at each other's throats in the distant reaches of the frontier. French trappers and traders came down the St. Lawrence River from Canada, across the Great Lakes, and down the Mississippi and Ohio rivers to reach the back country of New York, Pennsylvania, Maryland, and

97

Early trapping equipment from New York State. The Dutch who settled New Amsterdam pushed up the Hudson River to tap the Indian sources of furs. *Courtesy, The Farmers' Museum, New York State Historical Association, Cooperstown, N.Y. Photograph by Frank Rollins.*

Virginia, where they stirred up the Indians against the English settlers. Many Frenchmen became trappers themselves, *coureurs de bois* ("woods runners"), married Indian squaws, and in time were hardly distinguishable from the Indians.

The Dutch who settled in New Amsterdam, later New York, were not far behind in their zeal to tap the great Indian fur supplies on the rivers and streams of the interior. Soon after New Amsterdam was settled in 1624, Dutch traders were pushing up the Hudson River to the present site of Albany and beyond. English traders from New England competed with Dutchmen in the backwoods of Connecticut, New Jersey, and Pennsylvania. The fur trade was an important business in all the colonies throughout the colonial period, and for more than a century after independence it continued to attract some of the most adventurous men in American history.

During the late seventeenth century, men like William Byrd I of Virginia sent traders up the rivers into the Appalachian Mountains and across into the great valleys beyond. Long before Daniel Boone, these daring traders made contact with the Indians, with whom they bartered pots, pans, and blankets, and sometimes rifles, ammunition, and rum, for the furs that were in such great demand in European markets—furs that helped to make rich more than one colonial family.

Even in the Far South the fur trade was important, but furs such as beaver and mink, which constituted most of the traffic farther north, were supplanted by deerskins. Deerskins were highly prized abroad for gloves; domestically, the skins were used for jackets, breeches, and other wearing apparel.

In the Carolinas, many of the traders were hard-bitten Scotsmen, who followed well-worn Indian trails into the mountains where they found the Cherokees and other Indian tribes eager to barter their deerskins for the white man's wares. Charleston merchants outfitted traders, supplied them with trading goods and packhorses, and sent them off to the mountains. In the spring they returned, laden with deerskins, and made a rendezvous in Charleston. Sometimes they brought captive Indians whom the Cherokees, the Creeks, or the Chickasaws had taken in their tribal wars and sold to the traders. These luckless prisoners were shipped off to the West Indies as slaves to work on the sugar plantations. No Indian slave could be kept on the mainland, for he would contrive to escape and make his way back to the woods. These Carolina traders who came to Charleston each spring were tough and daring fellows, not unlike the mountain men who first ventured into the Far West. They were often greedy and ruthless, fearing neither man nor God, and their rendezvous in Charleston was certain to bring excitement and sometimes bloody fights.

The fur trade was of such importance to Great Britain, as well as to the colonies, that in the 1760's the government in London made strenuous efforts to regulate it and to keep the white settlers from encroaching on traditional Indian hunting grounds in the region beyond the mountains. The government was not concerned about justice to the Indians but about ensuring the continuance of a profitable trade. For this reason, in 1763, the English government drew an imaginary line along the crest of the Appalachian Mountains called The Proclamation Line and declared that white men should not settle beyond that point. But traders had brought back news of rich lands across the mountains and nothing could keep courageous pioneers from moving beyond the high hills that blocked their progress. The Proclamation Line merely irritated colonial Americans and helped to stimulate a spirit of rebellion.

5

Apprenticeship, Trade, and Getting Ahead in the World

An ambitious young man in America today—or woman, for that matter—has a choice of many careers. He is limited only by his innate ability and his determination to get the proper education and training for the career of his choice. Both private and state educational systems make an effort to see that anyone of talent, even if his financial resources are negligible, has an opportunity to develop to his full capacity.

Young people of the colonial period, however, faced a very different situation. The variety of careers was far less extensive than today. Professional schools of the modern kind were nonexistent. No schools of business administration were available to a young man who hoped to become a business executive. No business colleges offered training for girls. In fact, girls were not expected to go into business—though a few widows did take over their husbands'

101

An eighteenth-century woodworker's apprentice learned the "art and mystery of his craft" in a shop like this of the Dominy family of craftsmen of Easthampton, Long Island. *Courtesy, The Henry Francis du Pont Winterthur Museum, Winterthur, Del.*

trades. The colonial youth had to prepare for life the hard way, by way of an apprenticeship in some calling.

Apprenticeship is an ancient method of training; its origins are lost in the mists of time. The specific conditions and provisions of apprentice labor and training, however, as applied in colonial America, date from the regularization of the system that took place in the reign of Queen Elizabeth, particularly to a law called the Statute of Artificers, dating from 1563. Although rules varied in details from colony to colony, the conditions of apprenticeship throughout the colonial period varied little from those laid down under Elizabethan law. For example, an indenture (contract) from York County, Maine, dated 1674, could have been used with only a few changes in Elizabethan

England—or in any colony up to the time of the American Revolution. Only the term of service might have varied. In the York County indenture, the apprentice agreed to serve his master faithfully for a "full and just term of four years." He also agreed that he would keep any trade or other secrets of his master, that he would "not play at unlawful games, nor unseasonably absent himself from his said master's business; he shall not frequent taverns, nor lend, nor spend the goods or victuals of his said master without his leave." The apprentice contracted not to marry or to be guilty of any immorality. For his part, the carpenter to whom the Maine apprentice was bound promised to teach the lad "in the trade of a carpenter to the best of his skill according to what his apprentice is capable of, and also . . . to teach him to write and cipher if he be capable,

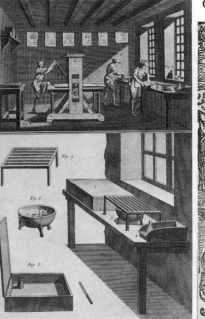

An eighteenth-century printing shop and the kind of equipment that Isaiah Thomas learned to use. *From the Folger Library copy of Diderot and D'Alembert*, Encyclopédie. Recueil des Planches (1751–65).

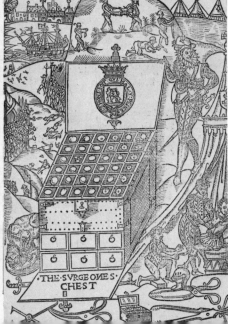

A surgeon's apprentice was required to learn the contents of a chest like this. Captain John Smith reported "Of our Chirurgians they were so conceited, that they beleeved any Plaister would heale any hurt." *From the Folger Library copy of William Clowes,* A Proved Practice for all Young Chirurgeons *(1588).*

and to give him a set of tools at the end of his time, and to provide him during the said apprenticeship convenient meat, drink, lodging, and washing, and seven pounds per annum for to find him apparel."

In essence, a master agreed to teach a youth "the art and mystery of his craft" in return for the youth's labor for a specified period of years. During this term of service, the master stood in place of a parent and could exercise the same authority as a father. That is, he could punish the apprentice for any infringement of the rules and could even beat him if his misdeeds warranted it. Punishments of apprentices were occasionally harsh, and numerous court records exist of masters charged with cruelty to apprentices and servants. We can be certain, however, that the authorities intervened only in cases of unusual severity, for beatings were considered normal. In 1666 Nicholas and Judith Weekes of Kittery, in what is now Maine, went too far,

In the days when shoes and boots, essential for riding and muddy roads, were all made by hand, shoemakers were eagerly sought. *From the Folger Library copy of Johann A. Comenius,* Orbis Sensualium Pictus *(1685).*

Planters were eager to have their own slaves learn skills necessary to a plantation. Here bayberry candles are being removed from molds by first immersing the mold in hot water, then gently pulling out the candle by its wick. *Courtesy, Colonial Williamsburg, Williamsburg, Va. Photograph by Thomas L. Williams.*

and caused the death of a servant. The wife confessed that she had cut off his toes. Occasionally the court intervened in the case of an unruly apprentice or servant. A Virginia jury in 1663, after considering a case of incorrigible impudence from a woman servant indentured to a master who could not control his household, ordered both servant and master to be ducked: she for impudence, he because he had "degenerated so much from a man as neither to bear rule over his woman servant or govern his house."

The apprentice lived in his master's house. In many cases he became in effect an adopted member of the family; frequently an apprentice, at the end of his service, married one of his master's daughters. In less happy cases, the apprentice might have the misfortune to be bound to a

Shipbuilding helped to create the New England economy. One of the subsidiary crafts it developed was the forging of anchors. *From the Folger Library copy of Diderot and D'Alembert,* Encyclopédie. Recueil des Planches *(1751–65).*

grasping and cruel master, who made him work long hours, gave him poor food, and beat him unmercifully. Even the best of employers made the apprentice's life a hard one, filled with work from dawn till dusk—with very little time off for amusement. Benjamin Franklin put into the mouth of Poor Richard the proverb: "An idle brain is the devil's workshop." Few colonial masters could be accused of being the devil's accomplices by encouraging idleness.

Although the sons of wealthy families—rich planters in the southern colonies and wealthy merchants in the North, for example—might be fortunate enough to enter one of the learned professions and acquire the necessary education in a university, or, in the case of law, at one of the Inns of Court in London, the almost invariable road to a business career or to a skill in some craft was by the apprentice route. Even well-to-do families saw to it that their sons were apprenticed to a master who could teach them a business or a craft. The daughters of the well-to-do were rarely apprenticed to any craft. They learned the domestic duties expected of a wife and married early. But girls of poorer families were often bound out as servants and apprenticed to some trade: needlework and sewing of various kinds, spinning, weaving, and various decorative arts. Some girls learned to be professional cooks, bakers, pastry makers, and sellers of prepared foods. Many a poor girl bound out under the apprentice laws became merely a household drudge doing the chores of an ordinary domestic servant.

Children were bound out as apprentices when they were very young. Normally, boys served a master until they were twenty-one; girls served until they were from sixteen to eighteen, or until they married. It had not yet occurred to anyone that child labor was evil, and children were expected to work as early as they could manipulate the implements of labor. Isaiah Thomas, who eventually rose to eminence as a wealthy printer in Worcester, Massachusetts, was apprenticed in 1756 at the age of six, before he had learned to read, to a rascally Boston printer named Zechariah Fowle. Young Thomas began his printing career by setting a broadside ballad entitled *The Lawyer's Pedigree* [*to the*] *Tune* [*of*] *Our Polly Is a Slut*. Thomas had a colorful career, amassed a fortune, and founded the American Antiquarian Society; but his entire education was gained behind the type case of a print shop. Children as young as the six-year-old Isaiah Thomas were apprenticed by their parents, who signed the indentures. Nobody in Thomas' day would have thought of blaming his parents for apprenticing him at so tender an age. When a child was presumed to know his own mind, he was expected to sign his own indenture, and if he could not write, he had to make his mark in the presence of witnesses. In the case of orphans, town or county authorities had the right to bind them out at any age to masters who would look after them and bring them up in some trade or occupation.

Choosing a trade was not always easy under the apprentice system, for master craftsmen did not want to train too many competitors. They therefore limited the number of apprentices by charging an entrance fee. Benjamin

In such Old World bakeries as these, colonial bakers of ship biscuit had learned their craft. *From the Folger Library copy of Bartolomeo Scappi,* Opera *(1605).*

Franklin's father wanted his son to learn the cutler's trade but was unable to pay the fee demanded by a master cutler. Young Ben therefore had to become an apprentice in a print shop—to the future benefit of his country. If Franklin had become a maker of knives instead of a publisher, the young nation would have lost one of its brightest stars. Upon such chances of Fate do the destinies of men and nations sometimes hang. Some crafts, for example, those of silversmiths and goldsmiths, demanded that apprentices come from prosperous homes with substantial financial backing. They theorized that after his seven years' apprenticeship a boy would not be able to set up shop as a master silversmith or goldsmith without capital supplied by his family.

Some of the professions that we regard as learned supplied their ranks from apprentices. For instance, physicians and surgeons in colonial America usually attained their skill—and their licenses—by serving as apprentices to a practitioner. A surgeon's apprentice held the instruments and helped hold the unfortunate patient during amputations and other operations. By carefully watching his master, the apprentice learned the crude techniques that prevailed in those times. The physician's apprentice rolled pills, mixed powders, and carried the doctor's bag of medicines and instruments. He picked up the technical language of the doctor, learned to imitate his mannerisms, and in time grew a beard and looked and sounded enough like a physician to obtain a license to practice.

Compared with modern concepts of working hours, leisure, holidays, and paid vacations, the life of a colonial apprentice was hard, monotonous, and dreary. He was expected to work from dawn to dusk and to keep busy in the evenings if duties in the household required it. He could not restrict his labor to any set number of hours per week, and if he had a respite on Saturday or a half day

Six years after Ben Franklin became publisher of the *Pennsylvania Gazette*, the *Virginia Gazette* began publication in a printing office like this one. *Courtesy, Colonial Williamsburg, Williamsburg, Va. Photograph by Thomas L. Williams.*

some other time he was more fortunate than most. On Sunday, if the household was pious—as it frequently was—the apprentice was expected to attend church service and to conduct himself during the rest of the day with decorum, if not with solemnity. He generally had some duties to perform, even on the Sabbath, and some apprentices complained about being forced by their masters to break the Sabbath by working. Moralists generally concluded that the apprentice did not commit a sin by working on Sunday if his master ordered him to do so: the master was considered the sinner. But that did not bring rest on the Lord's Day to the weary apprentice; it merely shifted the blame for his Sabbath-breaking.

The smiths were mighty men in the seventeenth-century world. Here three Dutch blacksmiths hammer a molten ingot into some useful shape. *From the Folger Library copy of Jacob Cats,* Alle de Wercken *(1657–59).*

Although the colonial apprentice's life was arduous, he had no basis of comparison with any other way of life. Normally, he complained little about his lot. Everybody was expected to work hard, and if anybody dreamed of idle hours that was only a dream, some fantastic vision that did not belong to this world. Leisure is a modern invention. Not even the wealthy had much leisure in colonial America, for the very mechanics of existence required a constant struggle. Nevertheless, the apprentice found some fun in his daily routine, we can be sure, and there was always time salvaged for pleasure, even a half day now and then to go fishing or to play ball on the village green. Life was probably no more tedious for him than it is for the tired youth of today who wears himself out trying to find amusements that delight him.

Even if in theory the apprentice's life was a round of duties that seemed unending, in practice it was often quite different. Another proverb asserted that "All work and no play makes Jack a dull boy," and we can be sure that colonial apprentices were ingenious enough to see that they did not become dull for this reason. Rainy days and rough weather often halted outdoor work and gave a respite from labor. Youths could find ways to put such occasions to good use. Holidays, election days, and muster days always provided opportunities for breaking the monotony of routine labor. Few apprentices were so unimaginative that they could not steal a little time for gaiety and deviltry. The probability is that the industrious apprentice of the colonial period got as much fun out of life as the modern boy does with all his leisure and gadgets.

The kinds of trades and crafts offering opportunities for youths varied in the different colonies. Although in the agricultural colonies of the South most of the population engaged in some form of farming, a few trades requiring skilled artisans flourished. Good carpenters and builders were always in demand and the supply was never sufficient.

111

The great planters were constantly writing to their agents in England to procure for them an able carpenter, a good brickmaker, or a skilled cooper (a maker of barrels and casks). Leather tanners and shoemakers were eagerly sought. Some of these craftsmen were brought over as indentured servants, that is, servants who agreed to work from two to seven years to pay for their passage. Even some schoolmasters came over as indentured servants. At the end of their terms they were free to work at their trades or to take up land as farmers. Most of those who came to the South eventually became small farmers and landowners.

The white craftsman in the South soon found himself in competition with slaves. Planters were eager to have their own slaves learn skills that could be applied on the plantations. From a good carpenter, brought over from London, let us say, the plantation slaves could learn the rudiments of the trade. Most of the great plantation houses of the eighteenth century were built with slave labor supervised by a master builder who made the design, aided perhaps by one or two well-trained carpenters.

White artisans were needed in the South to train the slaves, but once slaves had learned the crafts required on the plantations, the skills of the free workers were no longer essential. Although competition with slave labor made life difficult for free craftsmen in the agricultural colonies of the South, some craftsmen, particularly in such centers as Charleston, South Carolina; Annapolis, Maryland; and Williamsburg, Virginia, managed to succeed. But having attained a small store of capital, most of them became landowners and planters themselves.

The story was different in the trading colonies of the North, where opportunities existed for skilled craftsmen and artisans of many types to ply their trades and build up successful businesses. In New England, for example, shipbuilding and fishing attracted a large number of sub-

sidiary craftsmen such as shipwrights, carpenters, joiners, painters, blacksmiths, metalworkers, ship chandlers, bakers (of ship biscuit), ropemakers, sailmakers, netmakers, and a host of other trades connected with the sea.

Every port of importance in the northern colonies soon developed around it a cluster of industries essential to the growing commerce of the area. Boys no longer were restricted to the occupations of farming or fishing. They could apprentice themselves to scores of trades which promised good pay and a secure place in the commercial society that was becoming ever more prosperous. If a youth fancied a life of business he could apprentice himself to a merchant as a clerk or bookkeeper and he might hope eventually to become a prosperous merchant himself. In a new country with rarely enough labor of any kind, an

When New York was New Amsterdam. Note Dutch shipping in harbor and windmill in background. *From a seventeenth-century engraving in the Huntington Library.*

ambitious youth by thrift and diligence could expect to rise in the world and to become an employer of labor.

Benjamin Franklin is perhaps the best-known example of the apprentice who practiced all of the prudential virtues and rose to success. Beginning as an apprentice printer in Boston working for his half brother, he left Boston in 1723 when he was seventeen for the more enticing opportunities in Philadelphia, already the most exciting city in English America. When he arrived he had one shilling and a Dutch dollar in his pocket. But a printer, even one only seventeen years old, could find work, and he got a job with an eccentric printer and publisher named Samuel Keimer. A letter that Franklin wrote to his family in Boston, telling why he had run away to Philadelphia, came to the notice of the Governor of Pennsylvania, Sir William Keith. The

Governor was so impressed that he went to Keimer's shop, made the acquaintance of young Franklin, and sent him to London to perfect his trade. On his return from England, Franklin worked for a Quaker merchant, where he learned the art of salesmanship and bookkeeping; but soon he was practicing his trade of printer again with Keimer. Later, in 1730, Franklin became the owner of a printing establishment and the publisher of the *Pennsylvania Gazette*, which he made the most interesting newspaper in the colonies.

In his *Autobiography* Franklin described with complacent pride his rise to success and pointed the way for others to follow in his footsteps. He confessed honestly that vanity prompted him a little in writing his *Autobiography* and added:

Most people dislike vanity in others whatever share they have of it themselves, but I give it fair quarter wherever I meet with it, being persuaded that it is often productive of good to the possessor and to others that are within his sphere of action, and therefore in many, many cases it would not be quite absurd if a man were to thank God for his vanity among the other comforts of life.

Franklin's self-confidence was characteristic of the typical young man in colonial America who was certain that by his own diligence he could attain success.

Franklin's *Autobiography* and *Poor Richard's Almanac*, which he published from 1732 to 1757, provided advice on how to get ahead in the world and are foundation stones in the cult of success that has dominated American thinking from that day to this. Franklin wrote:

In order to secure my credit and character as a tradesman, I took care not only to be in reality industrious and frugal, but to avoid all appearances to the contrary. I dressed plainly; I was seen at no places of idle diversion. I never went out a-fishing or shooting; a book, indeed, sometimes debauched me from my work, but that was seldom, snug, and gave no scandal. And to show that I was not above my business, I sometimes brought home the papers I purchased at the stores through the streets on a wheel-

I can not gi the
dirte & past of
my hands

The techniques and equipment of baking, as of other crafts, were transplanted to the colonies from England or the continent. This "beehive" oven is a larger model of many found in colonial kitchen fireplaces. *From T. F., "A Book of Divers Devices" in the Folger Library manuscript collection.*

barrow. Thus being esteemed an industrious, thriving young man and paying duly for what I bought, the merchants who imported stationery solicited my custom, others proposed supplying me with books, [and] I went on swimmingly.

Many apprentices, before and after Franklin, exemplified the doctrines of diligence, thrift, sobriety, and incessant attention to business that Franklin's almanacs advocated. In the preface to *Poor Richard Improved* (1758), Franklin summed up his advice on getting ahead in an essay that has since become known as *The Way to Wealth*. Few other American works have been so often reprinted and so widely translated abroad. In it the author epitomized his own philosophy of prudence and thrift that would lead inevitably, readers confidently believed, to material prosperity. In conclusion, Franklin advised his readers

116

not to "depend too much upon your own industry and frugality and prudence, though excellent things, for they may all be blasted without the blessing of Heaven, and therefore ask that blessing humbly. . . ." If one followed the advice to live frugally, prudently, industriously, soberly, without extravagance, and at the same time sought Heaven's blessing, one could scarcely fail to succeed in the accumulation of material assets. There would be little else for one to do.

One of the early examples of the successful American who attained prosperity by following the practices that Franklin codified in *The Way to Wealth* was John Hull, son of a substantial blacksmith, who brought him to Massachusetts Bay in 1634. By the time he was eighteen, Hull, an apprentice goldsmith and silversmith, was already an accomplished artisan. He developed into one of the most skillful craftsmen of his time in Boston, where he turned

A colonial Virginia bakery of the kind that helped to make the Cockes wealthy. Note the long-handled paddle and oven similar to those in the preceding English drawing. *Courtesy, Colonial Williamsburg, Williamsburg, Va. Photograph by Thomas L. Williams.*

out handsome pieces of silver for anyone who could afford to buy them. Indeed, Hull was the instructor of other silversmiths who made Boston silver notable at the end of the seventeenth and beginning of the eighteenth centuries.

So skillful was Hull that he became master of the mint in Massachusetts Bay Colony, and he and his partner, Robert Sanderson, were the coiners of the "pine-tree shillings," so called from the design on the coin. As Hull's prosperity increased, he extended his business dealings into other fields until he was the owner of a splendid house in Boston, of farm lands in the nearby country, and of ships trading far and wide.

Hull's rise to wealth and respect in Boston was characteristic of many other colonial Americans. The Burrill family of Lynn, Massachusetts, illustrated the rise to prosperity of a whole dynasty known as "the Royal Family of Lynn." The first of the line was plain George Burrill, a farmer, who acquired two hundred acres of land in Lynn in 1638. His numerous progeny apprenticed themselves to sailmakers, shoemakers, maltsters, coopers, tanners, tailors, and other craftsmen and worked their way up the scale

French Huguenot silversmiths, such as the Revere family, had learned their craft in shops like this. *From the Folger Library copy of Diderot and D'Alembert,* Encyclopédie. Recueil des Planches *(1751–65).*

until they were master craftsmen and businessmen of reputation and wealth, playing an important part in the political and social life of the colony.

The rise of the Pepperrell family of Maine was as dramatic as the famous story of Dick Whittington, the apprentice, who became Lord Mayor of London. The first of the line in this country was William Pepperrell, a fisherman, of Sable Island, who moved to Kittery and married the daughter of a prosperous citizen. But his success was a result of his own diligence and ingenuity. He added merchandising to his trade of fishing and was soon selling supplies to other fishermen, shipping lumber in his own ships to the colonies to the south, and extending his trade to the West Indies and Europe. His son became a partner in the businesses. Like so many other American families, they invested their profits in lands until they became great landowners as well as rich shipping magnates. Young William Pepperrell became chief justice of Massachusetts and was commanding officer at the capture of the fortress of Louisbourg from the French in 1745, for which feat the King created him a baronet. From fisherman to nobleman of the British Empire was a great advance, but it did not seem improbable to ambitious young Americans of the eighteenth century, who regarded the world as their oyster which they could open by their own ingenuity and skill.

A success that stirred the romantic interest of New England boys for generations was that of William Phips, who served an apprenticeship to a carpenter and remained a ship's carpenter in Boston for many years. A marriage to the widow of John Hull, the goldsmith, brought him capital enough to expand his trade into the business of shipbuilding, and from shipbuilding to shipping. On a trading voyage to the West Indies in one of his own ships, he heard tales of Spanish galleons sunk with cargoes of gold in the shallow waters of the Caribbean. Phips came back to Boston fired with ambition to raise some of these treas-

119

ure ships and, unlike most treasure hunters, he actually found a galleon and salvaged the gold. So convincing was Phips about the possibility of finding gold that King Charles II in 1683 lent him a naval vessel and a little later the Duke of Albemarle interested himself in the venture.

Phips and his crew located a treasure ship sunk off Haiti and took from it enough gold and silver to make Phips wealthy and to reward richly both his crew and his backers. In 1687, James II, who had succeeded his brother as King, made Phips a knight. Sir William and Lady Phips, who in the days when Phips was a carpenter had yearned for a fine house in Boston, bought a mansion in Green Lane. Phips was later named royal governor of Massachusetts. But in his prosperity he did not forget his former associates among the carpenters and shipbuilders, and he sometimes scandalized the pious and respectable citizens of Green Lane by his association with unedifying companions. Nevertheless, Cotton Mather in his vast compilation describing godly New Englanders, the *Magnalia Christi Americana* (1702), characterized Phips's career as an illustration of God's blessings upon one who displayed "heroic virtues."

Massachusetts Bay and Boston had no monopoly of diligent and thrifty men who rose to positions of prosperity and eminence because of their heroic virtues in the market place. New York from its beginning was a place of trade and commerce where fortunes were made, first in the fur trade, and then in general commerce with the West Indies and Europe. Newport and Providence, Rhode Island, were also important commercial centers. The Brown family of Providence—founded by Chad Brown, a Baptist who combined preaching and business—during the eighteenth century became one of the most important merchant families of America. James and Obadiah Brown, who remained pious Baptists, in the 1720's and 1730's developed a pros-

Several styles of the much-favored Windsor chair in the Commons Room of the Red Lion Inn, originally at Red Lion, Del. The room itself is later than the colonial period. *Courtesy, The Henry Francis du Pont Winterthur Museum, Winterthur, Del. Photograph by Gilbert Ask.*

perous trade with the West Indies, where they exchanged corn, tobacco, cheese, shingles, pork, beef, and horses for sugar and molasses needed for their rum distilleries. After the British government placed an import tax on molasses in 1733, the Browns grew adept at smuggling—a violation of the British maritime laws regarded by most colonial shippers as a work of virtue. The dynasty of the Browns in Providence proved one of the most enduring and prosperous of all the colonial merchant families.

In Philadelphia, the Quakers were extremely successful as businessmen. They practiced the same virtues of diligence, sobriety, and thrift that characterized the Puritan traders of New England and succeeded equally well. With prosperity came a gradual weakening of the Quaker objection to luxury, and some of the great Quaker merchants of Philadelphia lived in handsome mansions, kept coaches and liveried drivers, and dressed in a manner that disturbed some of the stricter brethren. When Isaac Norris, one of the most affluent Quakers, bought a new coach in 1713, he balked at having a coat-of-arms painted on the door but settled for his initials and prescribed that his coachman should be dressed in something "strong and cheap, either of a dark gray or sad color." The activities of the Philadelphia merchants helped make that city the second in size in the whole of the British Empire in the years immediately before the Revolution.

Even in the Deep South, planters did not despise trade and many of them added to their incomes by buying and selling. One proud Virginia family, the Cockes, made money by establishing a bakery to supply ship biscuit. Two of the most important families in South Carolina had their origins as artisans. The Manigault family began as carpenters. Gabriel and Pierre Manigault arrived in Charleston about 1695 with a little money. While working as a carpenter, Gabriel fell off a building and was killed. Pierre survived to prosper as a farmer, innkeeper, carpenter, distiller, barrelmaker, and merchant. By the time of his

Many a tall tale was told of marksmanship achieved with a Kentucky rifle. This Lancaster product became standard equipment for every hearth. *Courtesy, Old Sturbridge Village News Bureau, Sturbridge, Mass.*

death he had accumulated a comfortable fortune, and his son Gabriel became one of the wealthiest merchants and planters in South Carolina.

The father of Henry Laurens, one of the ablest leaders in South Carolina during the Revolution, was a saddler who became a trader and small merchant. Henry Laurens, his son, accumulated a fortune as a merchant and planter. Not even the most aristocratic of the planters in the colonial South despised trade. That attitude came in a later period of decadence. Colonial planters all knew that trade was important to their well-being and their prosperity.

The Manigaults and the Laurens families were typical of the Huguenot craftsmen who came to America to escape religious persecution in France. The Huguenots were Protestants who fled France after 1685 following the revocation of the Edict of Nantes, which had previously guaranteed them religious liberty. Among the refugees who settled in the cities of the Atlantic seaboard were some of the most skillful craftsmen of France. These included cabinetmakers, joiners, weavers, and silversmiths and goldsmiths.

Perhaps the best remembered silversmith of Huguenot descent is Paul Revere, whose famous ride to warn the patriots of the British march upon Lexington has given him a permanent niche in American history. But in various parts of the world there are connoisseurs of fine silver who never heard of the midnight ride and yet remember Revere for his fine craftsmanship, which he learned from his father Apollos Rivoire. Apollos came to America in the late seventeenth century by way of the island of Guernsey and apprenticed himself to John Coney of Boston. Coney had learned his craft from Jeremiah Dummer, who had himself been an apprentice of John Hull, the Boston mintmaster. So Paul Revere represented a long tradition in Boston of the fine art of silversmithing and related crafts.

Paul Revere was also typical of the ingenious and versatile type of American who could turn his hand to many things. Not only was he a talented silversmith whose handiwork brings fabulous prices from collectors today, but he was an engraver who designed the first paper money for the Continental Congress. He also made the first seal for the united colonies and the seal of the state of Massachusetts. He discovered a method of rolling sheet copper and made copper plates for the boilers of a steam ferry built by Robert Fulton. During the Revolution he was sent to Philadelphia to learn how to make gunpowder and for a time superintended a powder factory. As if these skills were not enough, he made false teeth and legend has it that he made a set for George Washington.

Many Huguenot refugee craftsmen settled in Philadelphia, which by the 1730's had become an important manufacturing center. Philadelphia was the source of much of the best colonial furniture; during the eighteenth century Philadelphia cabinetmakers and joiners produced furniture in such quantities that importations from Great Britain were greatly curtailed. Boston, Newport, Providence, New York, and Charleston were also places of manufacture of furniture, but Philadelphia led them all. Secretaries, chests, tables, bedframes, and chairs made of walnut, birch, maple, and even pine by skilled colonial craftsmen are collectors' items today and bring high prices. Colonial craftsmen imported the latest catalogues and pattern books from England and imitated the designs they found there, sometimes adding original touches. In general their work was characterized by simplicity, utility, and durability. Some cabinetmakers, however, achieved great beauty of design and their work attained high artistry.

Colonial craftsmen made a great success of two objects that had an enormous importance in the settlement of America, the so-called Kentucky rifle and the Conestoga wagon. For the development of both products, we owe a debt to German, Swiss, Huguenot, and other craftsmen working in Lancaster, Pennsylvania, a town founded about 1730 some sixty miles inland from Philadelphia on Conestoga Creek. A Swiss named Peter Leman had a forge in Lancaster County as early as 1721 and was making a long-barreled, small-bore rifle of great accuracy. Other gunsmiths in the area began making long rifles that were a vast improvement on large-bore European guns. Within a short time Lancaster rifles were famous throughout Pennsylvania and the neighboring colonies. With these rifles frontiersmen could hit a squirrel in the highest tree, or what was better, hit so close that the concussion stunned the squirrel long enough for it to fall and be caught without any bullet damage. Feats of marksmanship with these rifles became legendary, and they helped settlers to claim the West from the Indians. So useful were they in Kentucky that they came to be known by the name of that territory.

The Conestoga wagon, also a creation of Lancaster craftsmen, was important for inland commerce and movement into the interior. Its stout, high wheels made it pos-

A loom like this was a cumbersome but necessary piece of furniture in many a colonial cottage. *Courtesy, The Farmers' Museum, New York State Historical Association, Cooperstown, N.Y. Frank Rollins photograph.*

Almost every farmer's wife had a spinning wheel. This one is for flax. *Courtesy, The Farmers' Museum, New York State Historical Association, Cooperstown, N.Y.*

sible to traverse the roughest roads, and its capacious bed with high sides and a canvas cover protected the load from the weather. In these covered wagons farmers hauled grain and other produce to the Philadelphia market, and in them settlers carried their household goods into the great interior valleys beyond the mountains. This sensible vehicle brought prosperity to Pennsylvania wagonmakers and provided a needed means of transport into the interior.

In the back country of Pennsylvania the huge covered wagons, sometimes pulled by six horses, were used to carry cargoes of foodstuffs and home-manufactured articles over wagon roads to Philadelphia. Before the end of the colonial period Pennsylvania farmers had nearly ten thousand of these white-canvassed freighters which moved over the roads in fleets like land galleons, laden with treasure as important for the future of the country as the gold and silver of the Spanish treasure ships. From the port of Philadelphia this produce was shipped to other colonies in coastwise vessels and to West Indian and European markets.

This trade brought prosperity to many farmers and riches to a few merchants and traders. One of the most fascinating business magnates of the late colonial period who profited from back-country enterprise was Isaac Zane, Jr., son of a prosperous Quaker craftsman of Philadelphia, who developed a complex of industries and enterprises on Cedar Creek, south of Winchester, Virginia, in the Shenandoah Valley. His first great enterprise was an iron mine, smelter, and forge that produced bar iron and such finished iron products as the enormous kettles for scalding hogs, smaller utensils, plows, and other farming implements. By wagon he freighted most of this iron work to Georgetown, Alexandria, or Falmouth, Virginia for shipment to other colonies or overseas.

A seventeenth-century leatherworking shop. The two men outside are winding cord. *From the Folger Library copy of Johann A. Comenius,* Orbis Sensualium Pictus *(1685).*

But an ironworks was not the only activity of Colonel Zane, as he came to be called. He operated a distillery, a grist mill, a lumber mill, and a vast farm which produced foodstuffs for his laborers as well as a surplus to sell. And Colonel Zane, having risen to wealth and importance from his simple Quaker background, lived in un-Quakerlike luxury and grandeur. Here was a man who was a precursor of many a self-made American magnate of a later period.

Leatherworking was another of Lancaster's important trades, as it was in many colonial towns, for leather was an essential commodity. Leather was necessary for shoes, for breeches and jackets, for harness and saddles, and for various other uses. In a country where cattle abounded, a cow's hide was frequently more valuable than a carcass of beef. Farmers often operated tanneries and employed apprentices to tend the stinking vats where hides soaked in tanbark solutions until they were pliable. Numerous oak trees supplied the bark needed for tanning leather. Sometimes the same farmer who produced and tanned the hides also turned leatherworker and made saddles and harness. More often, however, such leatherworking was a specialized craft that flourished in the frontier regions where leather equipment was in great demand and brought a good profit.

Weaving was a cottage industry that flourished among the German settlers in Pennsylvania as well as among other colonial people. Pennsylvania textiles were an important commodity in the eighteenth century, but Pennsylvania had no monopoly of this industry. Almost every farmer's wife had a spinning wheel and many a farmer worked at a loom during the winter when little work could be done outdoors.

To an extent difficult for a twentieth-century person to comprehend, the individual family in many of the colonial regions was self-sustaining. This was less true in the tobacco-growing colonies, where a valuable cash crop provided, even for small farmers, the means of buying commodities overseas. Robert Beverley, for example, complained in *The History and Present State of Virginia* (1705) that his fellow countrymen imported nearly everything they used, even to their woodenware. But conditions were different in the colonies to the north, where no one source supplied cash enough to exchange for all essential commodities. Consequently, farmers trained themselves from the beginning to produce as many of their needed commodities as possible. Not only did they make textiles for their clothing, furniture for their homes, and implements for their farms and handicrafts, but they frequently produced a surplus for sale. The cottage industries of the North, as in England, were an important factor in the development of manufacturing.

Ideally Great Britain had hoped to be the source of manufactured products needed by the American colonies and had made laws to foster the production of raw materials overseas and the manufacture of finished products at home. In actuality, the colonies soon discovered that they could make many of the products that they required in daily life. As Isaac Zane's enterprise illustrates, even such basic industries as the production of iron had a beginning in colonial America. Earlier than Zane, Governor Spotswood of Virginia successfully operated an iron mine near Fredericksburg; Robert Carter of Nomini Hall had an interest in an ironworks in Maryland; and an important ironworks developed at Saugus, Massachusetts.

The natural resources of colonial America were unlimited, and opportunities lay waiting for any young man with ingenuity, imagination, and diligence. It is not surprising that so many successful enterprises developed once the first stages of settlement in the wilderness were over. To get ahead in the New World required hard work, but an ambitious youth found here no caste-bound society to hinder him and few laws that would thwart his endeavors. Opportunities were as unlimited as were the resources of the new country. Only the supply of labor was scarce, and that was an advantage to the young man whose only stock-in-trade was the work that he was ready to perform.

6

Schools and Learning

Every child born in the United States today can expect a free education provided by the taxpayers, and parents have come to regard as a natural right the education of their children at public expense. Every state in the Union now provides free education through high school, and some states provide free tuition at state-supported colleges and universities.

To our colonial ancestors, such bounty would have been unbelievable, a fantastic dream of Utopia. No colonial child, not even the child of the richest parents, had educational opportunities equivalent to those now available to the poorest citizen, and only a few colonial children were so fortunate that they could look forward to years of learning in school, followed by college and university. The natural condition of the majority of colonial children was one of hard work, with such smatterings of education as they

Schooling began, and sometimes ended, with religious instruction at home. Father was usually schoolmaster, as few women were educated. *From the Folger Library copy of* The Whole Book of Psalms *(1563).*

could get, depending upon their social status and the opportunities offered in their particular localities.

That is not to say that colonial parents were not concerned about the education of their children, for many of them were eager for their offspring to get at least the rudiments of learning, but schooling was neither easy nor cheap, and parents in many regions of the colonies found it difficult or impossible to send their children to school.

And yet the belief was general that children must learn to read and write, at least to read the Bible. Indeed, the necessity of being able to read the Bible was one of the great motivations for schooling among Protestant people. The key to salvation, Protestants believed, was to be found in the individual's reading of the Scriptures, and in order to have this key, everyone needed enough education to make the Bible accessible. After the Reformation in Scotland, for example, ministers of the gospel spread the doctrine that all must read the Bible or stand in danger of damnation. In two generations, someone has said, the fear of hell did more to civilize the Scots than all the laws that their rulers had previously made. The Scots became a Bible-reading nation in which schooling was a religious obligation.

This same attitude, which prevailed in many parts of the American colonies, helps to explain the efforts that parents made to teach their children at least enough to read the Bible. Masters of apprentices were required to see that their charges learned to read and to cipher (that is, to do simple arithmetic). In towns and thickly populated areas, schools were established; in the agricultural colonies, where farms and plantations were widely separated,

The most famous contemporary English grammar school, still standing at Stratford-upon-Avon, Warwickshire. Here William Shakespeare is assumed to have gone "creeping like snail/ Unwillingly to school." Colonial one-room schools, though smaller, probably looked much like this. *Courtesy, The Shakespeare Birthplace Trust, Stratford-upon-Avon.*

schools were few and parents made such shifts as they could to teach their children. Well-to-do parents hired tutors for their children and sometimes shared their services with neighbors. Less fortunate folk in backwoods regions might have to do without schooling or get what they could from itinerant schoolmasters and circuit-riding parsons.

The education of the Indians, curiously, was much on the minds of some of the promoters of colonization in the

Boys with their master, girls in "dame school" and "recess." *Frontispiece to Dilworth's* New Guide to the English Tongue *as reproduced in George Littlefield,* Early Schools and Schoolbooks *(1904). Folger Library copy.*

early days, and the foundation of some of the first schools was related to a missionary zeal to save the souls of the Indians and educate them in a civilized way of life. From the first, some Englishmen were troubled in their consciences about taking land from the Indians and argued about whether it was right to do so. According to one view, the heathen Indians were children of the devil, and Christians were justified in annihilating them and in appropriating their land. But a more charitable view was generally accepted that they were children of light only waiting for the Word of God to bring them to salvation, and that it was the duty of the colonists to teach them to read the Bible and to learn Christian ways.

The first educational enterprise in English America had the double purpose of educating the Indians and of providing facilities for the colonists. In 1619 King James himself instructed the bishops of his realm to raise money in their dioceses to found a university at Henrico in Virginia not far from Jamestown which would have a "college for the conversion of infidels." The Virginia Company of London, which controlled the colony, set aside ten thousand acres for the university and a thousand acres for the Indian college and raised money for the enterprise. Unhappily, the "infidel" Indians rose on Good Friday, 1622, and slaughtered hundreds of the Virginia colonists. This massacre not only dimmed the enthusiasm for educating the heathen but it also destroyed the undertaking completely. The University of Henrico, destined to be the first English educational institution in America, never developed.

Despite the fact that Virginia plantations were widely scattered along its waterways, some efforts were made in the first century of development to found schools and to provide for the education of those families too poor to hire private tutors. As early as 1635 a Virginia planter named Benjamin Symmes bequeathed two hundred acres of land and eight cows to establish a school for the children of

135

Elizabeth City and Kecoughtan. A few years later a planter named Thomas Eaton established another school at Elizabeth City. Both Symmes's and Eaton's schools lasted until the nineteenth century. Many planters provided sums of money in their wills for the education of poor children sufficient to enable them to read the Bible; and schools run by itinerant schoolmasters, sometimes called "old field schools," provided some measure of instruction. The well-to-do planters who found it difficult to hire private tutors sometimes sent even their small children to England to be educated. For example, William Fitzhugh, a planter in what was then a backwoods area of Stafford County, Virginia, in 1690 was contemplating sending his son and heir, then aged four, to London for schooling when a French Huguenot minister came to Stafford and agreed to tutor the child in lessons that included both Latin and French. Finally, when young William was little more than eleven years old, Fitzhugh sent him to England in care of his agent at Bristol who looked after his tobacco shipments. The lad was to be placed in a school where he would have good instruction in Latin; in addition to supervising his intellectual welfare, the agent was instructed to provide him "now and then a little money to buy apples, plums, etc." Young William Fitzhugh did well, learned Latin and other things, ate his apples and plums, and eventually returned to Virginia to become a leader and an ornament to the colony.

In closely settled regions like New England, the township governments accepted the responsibility of providing for the education of children. Since the population was concentrated, pupils could get to centrally located schools by walking if no other transportation was available. Our ancestors had not yet lost the use of their legs, and many a colonial child thought nothing of walking three or four miles to get to a village schoolhouse.

The settlers of Massachusetts Bay were determined that

136

no child should be without benefit of at least the fundamentals of learning, and the General Court passed a law in 1642 instructing officials of every township to see that parents and the masters of apprentices gave children in their care education enough to insure "their ability to read and understand the principles of religion and the capital laws of the country." Another act passed in 1647 warned everyone against the wiles of "that old deluder Satan," whose purpose was "to keep men from the knowledge of the Scriptures." Hence it was important to defeat the devil by requiring every town that had as many as fifty householders to hire a teacher who would instruct all the children of the community in reading and writing. Revision of the laws from time to time strengthened the requirements for teaching reading and writing.

The schoolhouses of the day were usually single-room

An early hornbook containing the Lord's Prayer. Thus religious instruction was combined with the ABC's. *From the copy in the Folger Library.*

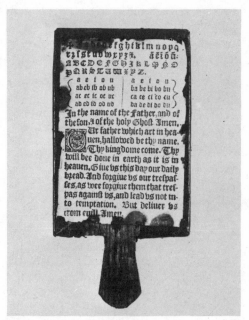

Where schools were not available, parents taught their children as best they could. It is easy to imagine the books being taken from the desk box in this corner of a farmhouse kitchen. *Courtesy, The Farmers' Museum, New York State Historical Association, Cooperstown, N.Y.*

structures where the teacher sat behind his desk on a raised platform and "heard the lessons" of the children of various ages and states of advancement. The youngest, just learning their ABC's, were equipped with "hornbooks," paddle-shaped pieces of board bearing a single leaf covered by a thin sheet of transparent horn to protect it from dirt and wear. This leaf contained the alphabet and a few simple sentences which the child learned to copy. Older children had readers and copybooks, usually with pious sentences, which they were instructed to copy and remember; thus they were expected to improve their handwriting and their conduct at one and the same time.

The lot of a schoolboy (or a schoolgirl, for that matter) was not easy, for teachers in the seventeenth and eighteenth centuries generally believed in exercising firm discipline enforced by a birch rod or a hickory switch kept in plain view to warn any would-be misbehaver of punishment in store. Not only were pupils soundly thrashed for disorderly behavior, but some teachers believed in "beating learning into them" when they seemed negligent of their lessons. The notion that school children might choose what they wanted to study and make a play of their work would have been regarded as heretical nonsense by colonial teachers. Punishments were sometimes severe, and many a youngster went home with the marks of the switch upon his legs. Parents for the most part approved of this discipline and it was the rule in some households that a child received another beating for good measure when he got home to signify the parents' approval of the punishment meted out at school.

Beating was not the only punishment. In some New England schools parents were expected to help pay for the child's education by supplying firewood; when parents failed to supply wood, their children were placed farthest from the fire in the coldest part of the room. A shivering child would be certain to carry the word home that wood was needed. Nobody worried about any complexes that a child might develop from being singled out for punishment.

Teachers were usually men, but women kept some "dame schools" for the youngest children, both boys and girls, and taught them their ABC's and the first steps in reading and writing. A widow might eke out a living by taking pupils into her house for instruction. Occasionally women kept schools for older girls and provided instruction not only in reading, arithmetic, and deportment but sometimes in Latin and French.

Elementary schools, sometimes called "English schools," taught simple reading, writing, and arithmetic—the three R's regarded as essential to anyone. But for further education in preparation for one of the learned professions one had to go first to a grammar school for the rudiments of Latin.

Massachusetts Bay, with a large group of university men

in its population, sought early in its development to provide adequate grammar schools where those who wanted a university education could get the necessary preparation. The General Court in 1647 declared that every town of a hundred householders should set up a Latin grammar school. Although many towns neglected to obey this injunction, it is worth noting that the authorities made a strenuous effort to ensure that boys of "hopeful promise" would have an opportunity of learning.

One of the most famous of American schools, important to this day, had its beginning in 1636 when some citizens of Boston hired a schoolmaster to teach Latin in what soon became known as the Boston Latin School. Other towns set up similar schools and soon New England had enough grammar schools to supply candidates for the university.

Although New England led the other colonies in the number and quality of its schools, some provision was made everywhere for the education of the young. Emphasis was upon the three R's, but here and there grammar schools and academies were established to provide something beyond the ability to read and cipher.

The least enthusiasm for education was displayed by the German sectarians of Pennsylvania, who were suspicious of too much book learning. Only the Moravians among the German immigrants and a few of the early Mennonites showed a concern about learning. The more extreme sectarians were content if their children knew enough to spell out German Bible verses.

The Quakers of Pennsylvania also lacked enthusiasm for book learning, but, being practical folk, they knew that illiteracy was a handicap and sought to eliminate it in the population of that colony. William Penn's First Frame of Government ordered the creation of public schools so that "all children within this province of the age of twelve years shall be taught some useful trade or skill, to the end that none may be idle, but the poor may work to live, and the rich, if they become poor, may not want." This practical aim of education was characteristic of the colonial Quakers. Although the majority were content with ordinary literacy, the William Penn Charter School, which developed from the Friends Public School founded in 1689, gave Philadelphia an excellent Latin grammar school.

The Quakers' insistence upon practical education and the importance of Philadelphia as a commercial center resulted in the establishment there of many private schools which taught such useful subjects as navigation, bookkeeping, and surveying, and, for women, needlework and other handicrafts. As a great port, Philadelphia had people who had sailed the seven seas and had heard strange tongues in the ports of the world. Enough residents of Philadelphia were aware of the need to learn some of these foreign languages to create a demand for language instruction. In the eighteenth century Philadelphia offered the best opportunities in the colonies for the study of modern foreign languages. Teachers advertised in the Philadelphia papers and found enough pupils to make such instruction profitable.

From the earliest days of settlement, a problem that worried serious colonists was some method of ensuring a supply of learned men, which any country, however new, needed. The Puritans in New England were especially concerned about maintaining an adequate supply of preachers, for it was not possible to send every boy who wanted to fit himself for the ministry to Oxford or Cambridge. Consequently, in 1636, a group of university men in Massachusetts, for the most part graduates of Emmanuel College, Cambridge, established a college to be a seminary of preachers, but more than that, a university for the instruction of laymen in the liberal arts. This first institution of higher learning in English America took the name of Harvard from its principal founder, the Reverend John Harvard. The author of a tract called *New England's First Fruits* (1643) describes the establishment of Harvard:

After God had carried us safe to New England and we had built our houses, provided necessaries for our livelihood, reared convenient places for God's worship, and settled the civil government, one of the next things we longed for and looked after was to advance learning and perpetuate it to posterity, dreading to leave an illiterate ministry to the churches when our present ministers shall lie in the dust. And as we were thinking and consulting how to effect this great work, it pleased God to stir up the heart of one Mr. Harvard . . . to give the one half of his estate (it being in all about £1,700) towards the erecting of a college, and all his library. After him another gave £300, others after them cast in more, and the public hand of the State added the rest. The college was by common consent appointed to be at Cambridge (a place very pleasant and accomodate) and is called (according to the name of the first founder) Harvard College.

The sons of the most prominent citizens of New England were soon coming to Harvard, and in time students came from elsewhere in the colonies. During the mid-seventeenth century some English fathers, thinking that Harvard offered fewer temptations and more godly surroundings than Oxford or Cambridge, sent their sons to New England to be educated, but most of these overseas students proved either so stupid or so ill-behaved that they left Harvard without graduating.

The curriculum was classical, with emphasis on the liberal arts as understood in that day: grammar, rhetoric, logic, Latin, Greek, Hebrew, mathematics, and astronomy. The influence of a new spirit of scientific inquiry was evident in the amount of time devoted to physics. Senior students concentrated upon metaphysics, philosophy, and divinity, which embraced a variety of theological studies. One of the college's primary purposes, one should never forget, was to turn out a number of young men trained to be preachers.

College life was a far cry from the comforts of modern collegiate existence; but since human nature is fairly constant, young men then as now had their fun, and not even

An English pencil sketch of a contemporary desk box. Writing materials and some books were kept inside and the sloping cover could be used as desk top. *From Halliwell-Phillipps*, Artistic Records, *Vol. 19, in the Folger Library.*

a Puritan environment could suppress the gaiety and the deviltry that go with youth. Students' quarters in the college buildings of the seventeenth and eighteenth centuries were sparsely furnished; a hard bed and a chest were usually deemed adequate. Some sort of washstand, with a washbasin and pitcher for cold water drawn from the college well, provided the only washing facilities, with an outdoor privy as the best "sanitary convenience." Fireplaces provided the only means of heat. Some parents helped pay their sons' tuition and other fees by supplying firewood, as well as other commodities such as corn and wheat.

Students had only two main meals, lunch at 11:00 a.m. and dinner about 7:30 p.m., with a menu very similar at both meals; boiled beef or mutton with bread and beer were the staples. But there were two other periods of refreshment called "bevers" at which the students were served bread and beer: one early in the morning, which we would consider breakfast, and one in the mid-afternoon.

The Great Building of the College of William and Mary, now known as the Wren Building, was built in 1695–98 from plans said to have been prepared by Sir Christopher Wren. It is the oldest academic building standing in the United States. *Courtesy, Colonial Williamsburg, Williamsburg, Va. Thomas L. Williams photograph.*

Beer was usual with all meals, though cider was common in later years. Water was thought unwholesome, and coffee and tea were unknown as collegiate refreshments. As Samuel Eliot Morison, the historian of Harvard, comments, "A draft of good sound beer, properly brewed and aged, is grateful to an empty stomach of a cold morning, or, for that matter, at any time of day, winter or summer; and the happy Harvard students of the Puritan century consumed it heartily at both meals and both bevers."

Harvard boys of the colonial period had their favorite places of resort where they could find additional refreshments and quench their thirst when the college commons did not supply enough. In the mid-seventeenth century a good woman named Vashti Bradish kept a tavern and bakery not far from Harvard Yard, and there the students flocked. When some busybody complained to the president of Harvard because she was "harboring students unseasonably spending their time and their parents' estate," the president, with the wisdom of Solomon, decided that Mrs. Bradish could continue to sell her bread and beer provided she served no one more than a penny's worth at a time and no one more than twice a week.

Our ancestors believed that hard work was more essential for a college student than recreation and rest; indeed the colonials were obsessed with the notion that one must not waste "God's precious time" but must spend every waking hour in the diligent pursuit of one's calling. Since Harvard had no bowling green, tennis court, playing field, or swimming pool, there were no organized sports, and the authorities would have looked askance at such affairs anyway. But since boys could not be cooped up in the college at their lessons incessantly, they occupied such leisure as they could find by strolling about Cambridge and its environs, swimming in the Charles River when the weather was suitable, or skating when the surface was frozen. Some found amusement in singing or playing some musical instrument. But the fear of wasting time kept many students from devoting much time to music. For instance, Josiah Flynt, a freshman in 1661, wrote to an uncle in London begging for a fiddle and received a reproving letter:

Music I had almost forgot. I suspect you seek it both too soon and too much. This be assured of, that if you be not excellent at it, it's worth nothing at all. And if you be excellent, it will take up so much of your mind and time that you will be worth little else, . . . unless you intend to take upon you the trade of fiddling.

The "trade of fiddling" in Puritan New England, we can be certain, was considered no worthy occupation for a university graduate.

College students were expected to appear in decent and

145

neat clothing and were forbidden to wear long hair. Harvard College's laws for 1655 state that

No scholar shall go out of his chamber without coat, gown, or cloak, and everyone everywhere shall wear modest and sober habit without strange ruffianlike or newfangled fashions, without all lavish dress or excess apparel whatsoever. Nor shall any wear gold or silver or such ornaments, except to whom upon just ground the President shall permit the same; neither shall it be lawful for any to wear long hair, locks, or foretops, nor to use curling, crisping, parting, or powdering their hair.

The authorities of Harvard, like others in the seventeenth century, showed a concern about the education of the Indians. President Henry Dunster persuaded a London group, the Society for the Propagation of the Gospel in New England, which had raised a large sum for the education of Indians, to contribute funds in 1653 for the erection of an Indian College in the Harvard Yard. Some cynics have suggested that Dunster was more concerned about getting a new building for his campus than he was about teaching the Indians of Massachusetts, but, be that as it may, a building was erected and in time a few Indians were brought to Harvard. The experiment did not prove a success. The young braves liked the beer and bread but they proved a disappointment when it came to learning Latin and Greek. One of the Indians, identified by Professor Morison as John Wampus, turned out to be a colorful character who took to drink and landed in jail for debt. Using his Harvard education to good advantage, he wrote out a petition to King Charles II asking royal intervention, and, surprisingly, in 1676 the King wrote to the Governor asking him to investigate. Unhappily for John, the authorities were obdurate, and he had to break out of jail and ship out to sea to escape the burdens of civilization.

Although the Indian College made no significant contribution to the education of the red men, one of its indirect contributions was the Indian Bible, translated in Algonquin by the missionary to the Indians, John Eliot. Eliot's Indian Bible was printed in the Indian College where the Cambridge printing press had found quarters. The translation of the Bible and its printing had been supported by the Society for the Propagation of the Gospel in New England, which had given the money for building the Indian College.

If Harvard was the first college and university in English America, it was not to remain the only institution of its kind. In 1693 the College of William and Mary was chartered and soon established at Williamsburg, Virginia, with the same general aims and ideals as those inspiring Harvard. The Virginians had also long worried about an adequate supply of ministers and learned men, and one of the aims of the College of William and Mary was to train

The living room of a house built between 1667 and 1678 on Long Island. Already some leisure was being found for books and learning. Note desk box with papers. *Courtesy, The Henry Francis du Pont Winterthur Museum, Winterthur, Del.*

preachers. The education of the Indians also played a part in the College's founding, and provision was made for an Indian College.

Although the College of William and Mary at first was little more than a high school, by May Day, 1699, the college had developed to a point where the authorities could stage a ceremonial occasion with five student orators to make speeches on the value of collegiate education in Virginia. Their orations, delivered before Governor Francis Nicholson, members of the House of Burgesses, and the principal citizens of the colony, were designed to impress the audience with the importance of the College. With the help of learning, one orator pointed out, Virginians would become familiar with excellent men of all ages—Plato, Aristotle, Cicero, and a host of other classical worthies— and, furthermore, the study of language would be a civilizing influence, for Virginians, living far from the centers of civilization, must struggle to keep their speech from growing corrupt. Another orator emphasized the value of an education in Virginia as opposed to one obtained abroad, for travel to "foreign parts" was difficult, dangerous, and expensive. Finally, one of the speakers declared that the purpose of education was to produce leaders needed by the colony and it was not designed to create pedants smelling of the lamp. The closing orator looked into the future and saw Virginia as a land of cultivation and learning: "Methinks we see already that happy time," he declared, "when we shall surpass the Asiaticans in civility, the Jews in religion, the Greeks in philosophy, the Egyptians in geometry, the Phoenicians in arithmetic, and the Chaldeans in astrology. O happy Virginia."

The education of the Indians at William and Mary was hardly more successful than that at Harvard, though the Virginians at least attempted nothing beyond high school subjects. Indian children were gathered up from neighboring tribes and brought to Williamsburg, where they were

148

boarded out in town and later lodged in the Brafferton Building. Many of them died of measles, whooping cough, and other diseases, and those who survived to return to their tribes lapsed back into savagery, sometimes with an accentuated taste for strong drink. Hugh Jones, a professor at William and Mary who wrote *The Present State of Virginia* (1724), commented that those who were taught to read and write, instead of becoming missionaries to their people, "have . . . returned to their home, some with and some without baptism, where they follow their own savage customs and heathenish rites." Efforts to educate Indians in colonial colleges were futile.

Yale, the third colonial college, owed its founding to a belief among some of the stricter Puritans that Harvard

Not all translations of the classics were "improving." This edition of Ovid's *Metamorphosis* was partially "Englished" in Virginia during the years 1621 to 1628 while George Sandys was serving as Treasurer of the colony. *From the Folger Library copy.*

was given over to modernistic and liberal ideas bound to lead to damnation. Conservatives, complaining that Harvard was a place of "riot and pride," asserted that the country needed a purer source of education for hopeful ministers and laymen. Some of these conservatives, all Harvard men, procured a charter in 1701 for a new college at first known as the Collegiate School at Saybrook. Not until 1716 did it move to New Haven. Supporters of the college remembered a New Englander, one Elihu Yale, who had gone to London and got rich as a merchant in the East India trade; they persuaded him to make a donation consisting of three bales of East Indian goods, a picture of King George I, and a parcel of books. When the sale of the goods realized £500, the authorities were so elated that they renamed the school Yale. Never was so much immortality bought so cheaply.

Other colleges were established in the eighteenth century. Princeton, founded in 1746, was designed as a seminary for Presbyterian ministers and was long dominated by Scotch Presbyterians. It had a tremendous influence later, sending out preachers and teachers to the frontier. King's College, later Columbia, founded in New York in 1754, was noteworthy for a rule forbidding the exclusion of "any person of any religious denomination whatever from equal liberty and advantage of education." The College of Philadelphia, later the University of Pennsylvania, which opened its doors in 1755, provided the most practical education in the colonies; it included agriculture in its curriculum and placed an unusual emphasis upon science. Brown University and Rutgers also had their beginnings in the period before the Revolution.

Professional education, except for the ministry, was left for the most part to apprenticeship or to training overseas. A considerable number of eighteenth-century colonials, including persons like William Byrd II of Virginia, received legal training in the Inns of Court in London. The best medical training was at the University of Edinburgh in Scotland, or Leiden University in Holland. But as early as 1765 the College of Philadelphia established a medical department. King's College in New York created a medical department in 1768.

In some fashion our colonial ancestors got an education, perhaps not much of an education, but enough to perpetuate a dream of better things and a desire for schools and learning. Where schools were not available parents taught their children as best they could. Although many children grew up illiterate, a surprising number of boys and girls in the most backward parts of the country learned at least enough to read and write. Only one segment of the population remained untaught. They were the black slaves. But

A pre-Revolution coverlet with scenes of Shakespeare and David Garrick, the great eighteenth-century Shakespearian actor. It was probably inspired by Garrick's famous Shakespeare Jubilee in 1769 and is an early example of Shakespeare's influence in America. *Courtesy, Old Sturbridge Village News Bureau, Sturbridge, Mass.*

even some of them picked up enough learning to read the Bible.

Learning, of course, is not a monopoly of schools. Then, as now, many people were self-taught. From the earliest days, books were imported and diligently read. Books in little colonial libraries for the most part were intended for utility rather than for entertainment. Colonial settlers, for example, brought along copies of William Barriffe's *Military Discipline, or, The Young Artilleryman*, which they thought, with good reason, they might need in learning to defend themselves against the savages. An extraordinary number of medical books, books on horse diseases, law books, works of piety, and books designed to tell how to get ahead in the world were part of the equipment that our ancestors thought essential to their well-being and advancement.

Sermons and godly handbooks made up a considerable portion of the libraries of all sorts of people, Puritans in New England and less puritanical folk in Virginia. William Byrd II of Westover, Virginia, certainly not a very pious character, nevertheless had many of the same religious books in his library that Cotton Mather, a very sanctimonious Puritan of Boston, cherished. All sorts of people, north and south, owned and read sermons and such guides to good behavior as Lewis Bayly's *The Practice of Piety*. Although pious literature was no monopoly of the New England Puritans, such works were particularly favored by this religious group.

Many a colonial youth received most of his education from reading. Benjamin Franklin provides in his *Autobiography* an explicit description of the self-education of a young man in the early eighteenth century. Son of a tallow candler and soap boiler of Boston, Benjamin could not afford to go to grammar school and college. Accordingly he went to a writing and arithmetic school where he learned enough for an apprenticeship in a printing shop. But that

152

was only the beginning of a long program of self-improvement. Though Franklin's father was a tradesman without much money to spare, he had a small collection of books which his son read avidly. Franklin wrote in the *Autobiography,*

From my infancy I was passionately fond of reading, and all the little money that came into my hands was laid out in the purchasing of books. I was very fond of voyages. My first acquisition was Bunyan's works in separate little volumes. I afterwards sold them to enable me to buy R. Burton's historical collections. . . . My father's little library consisted chiefly of books in polemic divinity, most of which I read. . . . There was among them Plutarch's *Lives,* in which I read abundantly, and I still think that time spent to great advantage. There was also a book of Defoe's called an *Essay on Projects* and another of Dr. Mather's called *Essays to Do Good,* which perhaps gave me a turn of thinking that had an influence on some of the principal future events of my life.

This early reading was merely the beginning of a long career in which Franklin was constantly improving his mind through books. He was instrumental in founding a subscription library by means of which he and his friends— all young men struggling to get ahead in business and trade —sought to remedy the defects in their education. "This library afforded me the means of improvement by constant study, for which I set apart an hour or two each day, and thus repaired in some degree the loss of the learned education my father once intended for me," he explained. "Reading was the only amusement I allowed myself. I spent no time in taverns, games, or frolics of any kind."

Self-improvement through reading, so clearly set forth by Franklin, became in America an important avenue to success. It was commended by others besides Franklin, and self-made men in the generations that followed frequently credited books that they bought and read with providing both the inspiration and the information needed for success. Some reading for sheer entertainment occurred, but most was "improving." A few "chapbooks"—cheap jest books, romances, and tales—provided light reading, but most books were serious informative works, translations of the classics, or pious tracts. Many small tradesmen and farmers—men like Franklin's father—had small libraries of useful books. A few large libraries existed. William Byrd II of Westover in Virginia had more than 3,600 volumes. Cotton Mather in Boston had a library of similar extent. A few town libraries were established. Booksellers in Boston, New York, Philadelphia, and other cities and towns imported books. The colonies kept up astonishingly well with current publications in London, and colonials were a reasonably well-read people. Self-education was playing an enormous part in the development of American minds.

7

Religion, Piety, and Sinful Deviltry

Few people living today can conceive of the all-enveloping influence of religion in the seventeenth century when our ancestors first began settling these shores. Religion touched every person's life, whether he was saint or sinner, and no man could avoid the impact of religious doctrines, whatever his personal views might be. Religion influenced laws and customs in all of the colonies, and in the Massachusetts Bay Colony and elsewhere in New England, religion was responsible for regulations affecting even minute details of everyday life.

The seventeenth century has been called an age of faith; it was at least an age in which countless men and women organized their lives around particular religious beliefs. Even some of the most worldly folk were connoisseurs of sermons and read pious books for both pleasure and instruction. Yet with all of their devotion to religion, our

155

The First Church, Boston, built in 1713 and razed in 1808. It is typical of the square Puritan meetinghouse that, after the turn of the eighteenth century, was often equipped with a small bell tower. *From the Folger Library copy of Samuel G. Drake,* History of Boston *(1853).*

colonial ancestors were often guilty of iniquities that caused the preachers to thunder against what they called "this sinful generation."

Fear of the wrath of God caused the most hard-boiled of seamen and ship captains to fall to their prayers, and the English explorers who sailed along the Atlantic seaboard brought along chaplains as a kind of insurance against disaster. Sir Francis Drake ordered regular prayers said on shipboard and forbade swearing lest it bring down punishment from heaven. Captain John Smith, for the same reason, prescribed punishment for profane swearers among the settlers at Jamestown. The first permanent structure that the Jamestown colonists built was a church, and provisions were made by the Virginia Company of London for the appointment of preachers to minister to the inhabitants.

The Old Chapel, Bethlehem, Pennsylvania, 1751. German Lutherans, like New England Puritans, preferred their church architecture, like their dress, severely plain. Steeples were considered "popish." *Photograph, Albertype Co., Brooklyn, N.Y.*

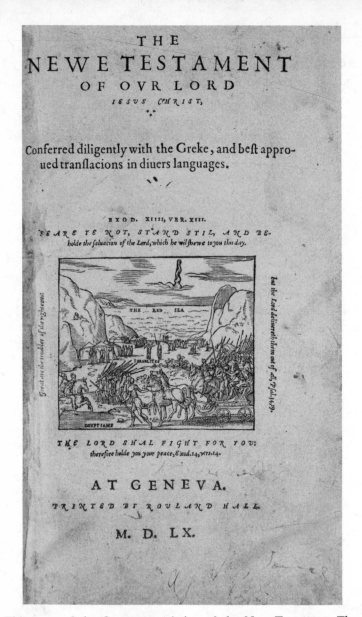

THE
NEWE TESTAMENT
OF OVR LORD
IESVS CHRIST,

Conferred diligently with the Greke, and beſt appro-
ued tranſlacions in diuers languages.

EXOD. XIIII, VER. XIII.

FEARE YE NOT, STAND STIL, AND BE-
holde the ſaluacion of the Lord, which he wil ſhewe to you this day.

THE RED SEA

ISRAELITES

EGYPTIANS

Great are the troubles of the righteous:

but the Lord deliuereth them out of all, Pſal.34,19.

THE LORD SHAL FIGHT FOR YOV:
therefore holde you your peace, Exod.14, ver.14.

AT GENEVA.

PRINTED BY ROVLAND HALL,

M. D. LX.

Title page of the Geneva translation of the New Testament. The Geneva Bible was brought to England by returning Protestant exiles after the accession of Elizabeth I. Conforming to the Protestant doctrine of individual reading of the Scripture, it was the first translation to be divided into chapter and verse, with headings, gloss, and notes, and the first to be printed in roman and italic, instead of black letter, type. It was, in short, the first layman's Bible and the Bible of most Protestant colonists. *From the Folger Library copy.*

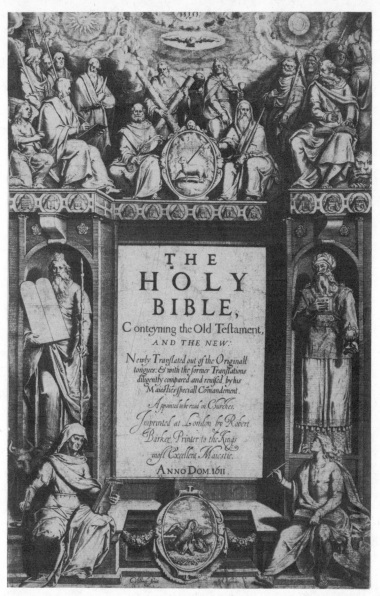

THE
HOLY
BIBLE,
Conteyning the Old Testament,
AND THE NEW:

Newly Translated out of the Originall
tongues: & with the former Translations
diligently compared and reuised, by his
Maiesties speciall Comandement.

Appointed to be read in Churches.

Imprinted at London by Robert
Barker, Printer to the Kings
most Excellent Maiestie.

ANNO DOM. 1611.

Title page of the King James Version of the Bible, published in 1611. Although this became the authorized Anglican text, many Puritan families in colonial America continued to use the earlier Genevan translation. *From the Folger Library copy.*

159

One of the motivations for colonization, loudly expressed by English propagandists for settlement overseas, was Christianization of the Indians. It was widely believed that conversion of these heathen would redound to the credit of England and insure a blessing upon the colonial enterprise. Enthusiasm for the missionary venture diminished in Virginia after the Indian massacre of the settlers on Good Friday, 1622. From this time onward many colonists argued whether Indians were children of light or children of the devil. If they were children of the devil, it was a virtue to exterminate them and take their land. In some quarters the doctrine prevailed that the only good Indian was a dead one. But that belief, expressed by colonists who had suffered at the hands of marauding Indians, did not eliminate efforts to convert the red men to Christianity. Learned men in London argued that the Church of England should see that the Indians were converted by their missionaries lest "popish priests" convert them to the Roman Catholic faith.

The settlement in Virginia was made by colonists who were, for the most part, members of the Church of England, and Virginia remained during the colonial period within the fold of the Anglican (Episcopal) establishment. That does not mean that no other faiths were represented in the population, but Anglicans predominated and it was the established religion of the colony. The same was true of South Carolina but before the end of the period the back country of South Carolina was filled with Scotch Presbyterians and some German Lutherans who had filtered down from Pennsylvania. North Carolina's population was even more diverse in its religious beliefs and included a substantial group of Quakers.

Maryland was first settled by Catholics sent out by Lord Baltimore, the Proprietor of the colony, who conceived the idea of establishing a refuge in America for persecuted members of his faith. To prevent objections from non-

160

Two Puritan governors. John Endicott preceded John Winthrop as Governor of the Massachusetts Bay Colony. *From the Folger Library copy of Samuel G. Drake,* History of Boston *(1853).*

Catholics, Baltimore decreed that Maryland would tolerate all Christians. In 1649 the Proprietor sent over a bill which became the law known as the Toleration Act, but this did not prevent the Puritans, who gained control for a time in the mid-seventeenth century, from passing an act in 1654 forbidding freedom of worship and taking away the right to vote from all who believed in "popery or prelacy." Fortunately this law was rescinded a little later, and by 1660 Maryland again tolerated all Christians. It included among its faithful many Anglicans who had come over from Virginia.

Clergymen for the parish churches of Virginia and other Anglican colonies were sent out from England after being ordained by a bishop, for not until after the Revolution was there a bishop in the English colonies. Not all of the ministers were an ornament to the church they represented. Some were lazy and others were more interested in acquiring land or in marrying a rich widow than in preaching the gospel. Few if any had an interest in preaching to the Indians. Nevertheless, though it was difficult to find ministers to fill the pulpits of Anglican churches, a goodly number came to the colonies and served faithfully and well. Their rewards were often meager; Virginia clergymen had to take their pay in tobacco, which they had to sell through some planter who could ship it to London. When tobacco prices slumped because of overproduction, the poor minister found himself virtually destitute. Understandably, enthusiasm for the ministry in Virginia was not high.

During the century after the first settlements in New England, religion held a dominant place in the life of those colonies, and it continued to be an important influence for generations to come.

No frivolous behavior was permitted on the Sabbath, but even the Puritans could not keep lace and ribbons from creeping into the women's Sunday dress. *From the Folger Library copy of Wenceslaus Hollar,* Ornatus Muliebris Anglicanus *(1640).*

The Pilgrims who came to Plymouth in December, 1620, were pious and earnest Christians willing to suffer for their beliefs. They had previously left England and had moved to Holland because they were unwilling to remain in the Church of England, which for them was too ritualistic. Known as "Separatists," they believed that each congregation should be independent, and this independent form of church government was the contribution that they made to the Congregational Church in America. They finally decided to leave Holland because they were afraid that their children would grow up with Dutch habits and customs and forget the faith of their fathers.

The Pilgrims were a small group in New England, but their history has made a lasting impression on the American imagination. We remember them because of their heroism during their first years, and for the institution of Thanksgiving Day. Indeed, the word "Pilgrim" probably brings to most Americans the picture of a soberly dressed seventeenth-century figure with a musket on his shoulder and a turkey under his arm, bringing home the essential item for Thanksgiving dinner.

Although the Pilgrims loom large in our imaginations, they were only a tiny minority among the New Englanders. The most important New England settlements were those made in the Massachusetts Bay Colony beginning about 1630. So numerous were the settlers who came in the ten years after 1630 that the movement is known as the "Great Migration." The Massachusetts Bay Colony was led by a group of Puritans headed by John Winthrop, an aristocratic English gentleman from Suffolk County, and Thomas Dudley, who had been the steward (or business manager) for the Earl of Lincoln and had accumulated a fortune himself.

The Puritans, unlike the Separatists, professed a desire to stay within the Church of England, but they wanted to "purify the church" by simplifying the ritual, eliminating the bishops, and altering some of its other customs and practices. Actually, once they were established in America, they broke their connection with the Church of England and became what we know as Congregationalists. They were a strict and stern group intent upon making over the church to suit themselves. The Puritan emigrants to Massachusetts Bay were determined to create a godly commonwealth, or a "garden of the Lord," where they could maintain the kind of religion that suited them best. Neither Winthrop nor Dudley had much tolerance for other religions and both were highly skeptical of too much democracy. They wanted a commonwealth in which godly leaders could control the multitude, and that is what they set up in Massachusetts Bay.

In the government of Massachusetts Bay, only church members were eligible to become "freemen," that is, citizens with the right to vote. And to become a church member, an individual had to testify that he had experienced

A nineteenth-century pencil sketch of ancient stocks in Warwickshire, England. *From Halliwell-Phillipps*, Artistic Records, *Vol. 18, in the Folger Library.*

The two arch-Puritan preachers of Boston, Increase and Cotton Mather. *From the Folger Library copy of Samuel G. Drake,* The History of King Philip's War *(1862).*

conversion; he then had to be approved by the minister, the church officers, and the congregation. This rigid procedure kept the government in the hands of a pious minority until later in the seventeenth century when the procedure for admitting freemen was modified.

In the early days of settlement, each New England community centered around its church with its minister as the chosen leader. Sometimes whole congregations would decide to move to a new location and would set out under the leadership of their pastor, driving their livestock before them. In that way many outlying regions were settled. For instance, the Reverend Thomas Hooker headed a group that removed from what is now Cambridge, Massachusetts, to Hartford, Connecticut, in 1636. Additional discontented Massachusetts Bay inhabitants removed about the same time to Windsor, Wethersfield, and other communities in Connecticut. Sometimes the authorities of Massachusetts Bay made life so difficult for those who disagreed with them that the dissenters had to leave. Roger Williams, a minister at Salem, aroused the enmity of the orthodox clergy in Massachusetts by questioning their interference in politics and made further enemies by questioning the right of the settlers to take land from the Indians. For these heretical views he was banished from the colony and had to flee to Rhode Island, where he helped to establish the most tolerant of all the New England colonies. The Massachusetts Bay Colony acted as a hive from which new colonies were swarming throughout the seventeenth century, frequently under the leadership of some clergyman who took his flock with him.

In the New England colonies the church usually occupied a central position in the town. Some strict Puritans preferred not to call the building a church because they maintained that this term brought back recollections of the "popish temples" they had left behind in England. The term that they liked best for the church was "meetinghouse." The typical Puritan meetinghouse of the seventeenth century was a plain square structure without a

The meeting of Macbeth with the three witches as pictured in Raphael Holinshed's *Historie of Scotland*, 1577. Holinshed's Chronicles were Shakespeare's chief historical source. *From the Folger Library copy.*

Frontispiece of *The Discovery of Witches*, 1647, by Matthew Hopkins, "Witch-finder Generall." Note the legal and Scriptural justification for witch-hunting. *From the Folger Library copy*.

steeple, for steeples also were regarded as "popish." Not until a somewhat later and more relaxed period were the meetinghouses equipped with bell towers that eventually evolved into steeples.

The earliest churches had rough wooden benches without backs. Men sat on one side and women on the other. Boys and girls were cautioned about making eyes at each other during the time of divine service and were supposed to keep their faces pointed toward the minister and to take no notice of one another. Later, when the communities had become better established, members in many churches were permitted to erect pews with high walls so that families could sit within the enclosed area and children could not see out and have their attention distracted.

Not until late in the eighteenth century did churches make any effort to provide means of heating. In the coldest weather congregations sat wrapped in their heaviest coats and listened to sermons that seemed endless. At times the cold was so severe that the communion bread froze, but that did not prevent the celebration of the sacrament and the lengthy sermon that went with it. Some church members brought along "foot stoves"—iron receptacles for holding hot coals—but these proved fire hazards which some churches forbade. Hot bricks or stones wrapped in old blankets also were used to add a little warmth to the arctic pews. But nothing much tempered the cold to the Puritans who listened and shivered as the parsons preached of the danger of hell-fire. The preachers' descriptions of the flames of hell must have given a cosy feeling to congregations half-dead with cold, who at that point were prepared to be less than terrified by fire and brimstone.

The preachers did not normally shorten their sermons to pamper their hearers, for they believed that suffering would chasten the spirits of sinners and add glory to the records of the saints. Sermons of two hours and longer were not unusual, and prayers could last an hour. Since the congre-

Belief in witches was not restricted to Britain or the colonies. This Halloween-like scene was published in mid-seventeenth-century Holland. *From the Folger Library copy of Jacob Cats,* Alle de Wercken *(1657–59).*

gation normally stood up to pray, an hour-long prayer must have caused a great deal of shifting and scuffling of feet. Cotton Mather reported that he prayed for an hour and a quarter at his ordination, and after that preached for an hour and three quarters. If it was hard to keep from freezing in the dead of winter during the interminable sermons, it was equally hard to keep awake in the heat of summer while the preachers droned through two or three hours of sermons and prayers. To prevent anything so untoward as a member falling asleep, a regular official of the church called the tithingman went around with a wand of office, a long rod with foxtails tied to one end. When women and

Despite all the laws and threats of hell-fire, human nature could not be utterly suppressed—except in the stocks. *From* The History of King Lear and His Three Daughters, *London, 1794. Folger Library copy.*

girls went to sleep he tickled their faces with the foxtails. Men and boys might be more rudely awakened with a punch or a tap on the head. When one sleeping church member at Lynn received a poke on the hand, he jumped up and broke up the service by yelling "Curse ye, wood-chuck!" He explained that he had dreamed that a wood-chuck had bitten him.

The Puritan Sunday or Sabbath was a time of piety and little else if the authorities could have their way. No work was supposed to occur on what the faithful preferred to call "the Lord's Day." Some towns interpreted the Scriptures to mean that the Sabbath began at sundown on Saturday night and they began strict observance at that time. The tithingmen of each congregation had the duty of reporting any violation of the Sabbath by man, woman, or child. No games were allowed, no frivolous behavior, no loud or raucous laughter, no fast walking or driving, no loitering outside the church on the Lord's Day. For any of these offenses the tithingman could caution the offenders, and for continued violations, the magistrates could sentence the guilty to be set in the stocks. One justice of the peace in Connecticut fined a couple of young people five shillings each because "on the Lord's Day during divine service they did smile."

Since young people were forced by law to go to church and sit through long sermons, it is hardly surprising that they were not always models of behavior. Unruly boys were often made to sit on the steps leading up to the pulpit in plain view of the whole congregation so that they could neither wriggle nor talk without attracting attention and reproof. Despite everything that the tithingmen and other adults could do, boys managed to cut and carve the pews and benches—just as schoolboys from time without end have carved their school desks. It is not surprising that whittling on the Sabbath was regarded as wicked. Nathaniel Mather, one of that clan of arch-Puritans, wrote that

When very young, I went astray from God and my mind was altogether taken with vanities and follies . . . Of the manifold sins which then I was guilty of, none so sticks upon me as that, being very young, I was whittling on the Sabbath Day, and for fear of being seen, I did it behind the door. A great reproach to God! A specimen of that atheism that I brought into the world with me.

Whittling on the Sabbath was bad, but what made it worse in the eyes of Puritan divines was that it was evidence of the wasting of God's precious time. Fear of wasting time was an obsession with the Puritans, who constantly preached against it. In a tract by Hugh Peter called *A Dying Father's Last Legacy* (1660), the author warns that "An hour's idleness is a sin as well as an hour's drunkenness."

171

The Virginia colonists were for the most part members of the
Church of England and, when Williamsburg became the capital,
Bruton Parish became the court church. It has been in continuous
use since 1715. *Courtesy, Colonial Williamsburg, Williamsburg, Va.*

172

Interior of Bruton Parish Church, restored to its colonial appearance. Across from the paneled pulpit is the canopied chair of the colonial governors. *Thomas L. Williams photograph.*

Mrs. Mary Rowlandson, who was captured by the Indian chief known as King Philip, reported in the narrative of her captivity that though she had formerly liked to smoke an occasional pipe, she refused to accept a pipe from her captors because it was evidence before God of a desire to waste time. She declared:

It seems to be a bait the devil lays to make men lose their precious time. I remember with shame how formerly, when I had taken two or three pipes I was ready for another, such a bewitching thing it is. But I thank God he has now given me power over it. Surely there are many who may be better employed than to lie sucking a stinking tobacco-pipe.

Judge Samuel Sewall of Boston was also concerned about the way children wasted their time, especially on holidays. In fact he was opposed to holidays in general because of this waste. Any celebration of Christmas he regarded as wicked on two counts, as he explained in his diary. It was a relic of "popish superstition" and it was a wicked waste of time better spent in doing something useful. As a matter of fact, in Puritan New England Christmas went almost unnoticed. Judge Sewall insisted that shopkeepers ought to go about their business on that day as on any other day. Celebration of the religious feast days, traditional in the Catholic and Anglican churches, the Puritans regarded as "idolatrous." Sewall wrote to a famous schoolteacher, the Reverend Ezekiel Cheever, on April 1, 1708, that he was much disturbed over the sinful vanities in the celebrating of stated anniversaries, and he had been particularly annoyed at children wasting time playing jokes on April Fool's Day. A child of six had told a worthy citizen of Boston that his shoes were untied and then had called out "April Fool." Sewall urged Cheever to bring up his pupils in a better way so that they would not thus waste God's precious time. "If men are accountable for every idle word, what a reckoning will they have that keep up stated times to promote lying and folly," he fumed. "What an abuse is

174

it of precious time! What a profanation! What an affront to the Divine bestower of it!"

The Puritans insisted upon ceaseless diligence in one's vocation, combined with sobriety and thrift. This combination of virtues explains why so many Puritan businessmen managed to accumulate fortunes. If they worked incessantly, stayed sober, and saved their money, they could hardly fail to achieve worldly success. Such success they believed was proof of God's favor and they were careful to see that their behavior would merit Divine benevolence.

John Hull, a famous Boston goldsmith and business magnate of the seventeenth century, gave written instructions to his ship captains to provide for religious worship on board every day so that the Lord would confer his favor upon them. "I know you will be careful to see to the worship of God every day on the vessel and to the sanctification of the Lord's Day and suppression of all profaneness that the Lord may delight to be with you and [shower] his blessing upon you, which is the hearty prayer of your friend and owner, John Hull," he wrote to one of his skippers. To another captain he warned that he must suppress Sabbath-breaking and swearing on board lest God send his vengeance upon them. These New Englanders regarded prayer and obedience to the laws that they deduced from the Old Testament as the best sort of marine insurance.

Many games that we consider too tame even for a Sunday-school picnic the Puritans regarded as wicked. The General Court of Massachusetts Bay in 1646 heard a complaint, for instance, about "the use of games of shuffleboard and bowling, in and about houses of common entertainment, whereby much precious time is spent unprofitably, and much waste of wine and beer occasioned." In consideration of this waste, the General Court forbade both shuffleboard and bowling. There was no objection to the drinking of wine and beer as part of any man's regular diet; the objection was to wasting these beverages in frivolity.

The Reverend John Cotton of Boston, one of the most revered ministers of the early days, was asked by a troubled father to rule on whether it was right for his daughters to draw valentines out of a hat, as was the custom of the time, and to dance. Cotton ruled learnedly that valentines themselves were not wicked, but that for girls to draw the names of young men, written on valentines, out of a hat was a lottery or game of chance, and this was equivalent to asking God to engage in a piece of frivolity. They might just as well take God's name in vain. Card play, involving cutting the cards, he would condemn for the same reason. As for dancing, he would not altogether condemn it because pious folk had danced before the Lord, as the Old Testament relates, but he would altogether forbid "lascivious dancing to wanton ditties, and in amorous gestures and wanton dalliances, especially after great feasts." Precisely what sort of dancing this worthy parson and others of his kind would expect from young people is not clear, for he implied that the only "mixed dancing" that he would favor would have to be religious in nature.

The parsons and the magistrates had difficulty suppressing all merriment, and by the later years of the seventeenth century a few dancing masters had the courage to open schools in Boston—not, however, without some interference. Judge Sewall noted in his *Diary* for September 17, 1685, that "Mr. Francis Stepney, the dancing master, desired a jury, so he and Mr. Shrimpton bound in £50 to January court. Said Stepney is ordered not to keep a dancing school; if he does will be taken in contempt and proceeded with accordingly." The constant warnings of the preachers against evil-doing must have created a strange sense of guilt in young people when they engaged even in innocent amusements.

A preacher, the Reverend Michael Wigglesworth, wrote the first American best-seller, a long poem entitled *The*

176

Day of Doom (1662), that must have terrified its readers young and old, for it gives a vivid description of the Day of Judgment when an Avenging Judge will sit on the throne of God and send sinners to the punishments they deserve. Under the stern Calvinistic doctrine that Wigglesworth and his kind taught, only certain elect of God, foreordained from the beginning of time, would achieve heavenly bliss. All the rest, including newborn babies, would be consigned to eternal pain in hell. But even Wigglesworth was somewhat troubled by this punishment for the non-elect among the infants; he made a slight concession for these innocent inheritors of the sin of Adam and has the Judge of All Creation give this sentence:

> A crime it is; therefore in bliss
> You may not hope to dwell;
> But unto you I shall allow
> The easiest room in hell.

The first edition of this poem quickly sold out and it was reprinted many times during the next century. Children were required to memorize long passages from it and to recite its warnings. What effect it had we can only imagine, but if modern psychological teachings about the dangers of terrifying children are to be believed, this fearsome poem must have been responsible for much mental disturbance in New England.

It is not impossible that the hysteria whipped up by *The Day of Doom,* combined with the emphasis upon supernatural interventions that were a constant refrain in New England sermons, helped to bring on the witchcraft hysteria that came to a climax at Salem in 1692. The belief in witchcraft was of course not confined to New England, but it had its most dramatic manifestations there. Two learned preachers of Boston, father and son, Increase and Cotton Mather, were largely responsible for the outbreak of prosecutions in 1692. Increase Mather had published a popular book called *An Essay for the Recording of Illustrious Providences* (1684), in which he had described strange supernatural happenings in New England, including the appearance of ghosts and apparitions, and the way demons could, and did, take possession of people. Increase's son Cotton heard about the children of a Boston brickmason, John Goodwin, who were reported to be bewitched, and took one of the Goodwin girls into his house so that he could study the case. The result of this clinical observation was another book, *Memorable Providences Relating to Witchcraft and Possession* (1689).

Since two of the most learned preachers of the time expressed their belief in demonic possession, the general public could not be blamed for accepting this authority as unquestionable truth. Belief in witchcraft had been deeply ingrained in the public consciousness many years before the outbreak in Massachusetts. King James had written a treatise entitled *Demonology* (1597) that had been republished in many editions. After the outbreak in Massachusetts, no eccentric person, no crotchety old woman or ill-dispositioned old man, was safe from accusations of witchcraft. By the beginning of 1692, the whole region around Boston was seething with talk about witches and demons, but Salem was a special center of supernaturalism. The preachers, particularly Cotton Mather, offered their services in stamping out the plague, and soon more than two hundred persons were accused. After twenty witches, both men and women, were hanged, and old Giles Corey, who refused to plead guilty or not guilty, was pressed to death by weights, according to an ancient English common law prescribed for those who would not plead upon their arraignment, the dreadful epidemic of fear ran its course. Some of those who had taken part, including Judge Sewall, later testified that they had been in error. But Cotton Mather wrote another book, this one in defense of the convictions at Salem, which he called *Wonders of*

LATE
Memorable Providences
Relating to
Witchcrafts and *Poſſeſſions*,

Clearly Manifeſting,

Not only that there are Witches, but
that Good Men (as well as others)
may poſſibly have their Lives ſhortned
by ſuch evil Inſtruments of Satan.

Written by *Cotton Mather* Miniſter of the
Goſpel at *Boſton* in *New-England.*

𝔗𝔥𝔢 𝔖𝔢𝔠𝔬𝔫𝔡 𝔍𝔪𝔭𝔯𝔢𝔰𝔰𝔦𝔬𝔫.

Recommended by the Reverend Mr. *Richard
Baxter* in *London,* and by the Miniſters of
Boſton and *Charleſtown* in *New-England.*

LONDON,

Printed for *Tho. Parkhurſt* at the *Bible* and
Three Crowns in *Cheapſide* near *Mercers-*
Chapel. 1691.

Title page of Cotton Mather's *Late Memorable Providences Relating
to Witchcrafts and Possessions*, 1691. This was the second edition,
published in London. *From the Folger Library copy.*

the Invisible World (1693). The Puritan clergy rarely doubted that they were the chosen instruments for conveying God's truth to the people.

Despite all of the strictures and laws against sin that the clergy and the magistrates could muster, human nature could not be utterly suppressed, and the records of the courts are full of convictions for all manner of violations of the laws of God and man. As New England became richer through trade and commerce, its ports were visited by sundry "wicked" people, and by the end of the seventeenth century, many of the inhabitants were no longer subservient to the clergy. During the eighteenth century worldliness and luxury increased, and religion no longer dominated every aspect of life. By the end of the colonial period, the Puritan clergy were fighting a rear-guard action, not only against worldliness, but against what to them was a greater danger: desertions to more relaxed faiths, the Anglican church in particular.

The stern and grim religion of the Puritans, so alien to the spirit of the modern world, bequeathed social doctrines that have had their influence upon later American history. We have not yet entirely abandoned the notion of the value of work as an end in itself. The belief that idleness is sin is deep-seated in the American character and helps to explain a persistent application to duty that has brought material success to many Americans. The Puritans were also convinced that they were the elect of God, the chosen people, and that doctrine too has helped to shape American character. Americans in general have found it easy to believe that we enjoy the especial favor of the Almighty and that our ways should be adopted by all other people. Perhaps that is a direct heritage from the Puritans.

The Puritans were not the only colonials whose religion profoundly influenced their lives. The Quakers who settled Pennsylvania were also convinced that religion could not be divorced from their daily existence. William Penn, the founder and Proprietor of Pennsylvania, himself was a Quaker who wanted his colony to be a haven for all oppressed people where they could live in harmony and achieve prosperity by their own industry.

Penn went through Germany, Switzerland, and Holland spreading the word about his colony and telling of the fertility of its soil and its freedom from tyranny of any sort. Soon immigrants from the Rhineland were swarming into the port of Philadelphia. Most of these settlers were people who had suffered from the constant invasions of their country, and they had become pacifists like the Quakers. The majority of the early German groups were Mennonites from Switzerland and the Rhineland, but other splinter sects came too, some of them with curious and strange beliefs. Later in the eighteenth century many Lutheran Germans came to Pennsylvania. The Germans pushed into the back country and settled on rich lands, where they became some of the most prosperous farmers in America. There they have remained to this day, living and believing much as they did in the seventeenth century. These "plain people" who wear black clothes and black hats and will have little to do with modern mechanical civilization are one element among the so-called Pennsylvania Dutch. Some of them even yet will wear no buttons on their clothes because in the eighteenth century brass buttons were symbolic of the military uniform, and they hated soldiers and soldiering. The elimination of buttons was one form of protest against militarism.

Penn's Quakers were among the most industrious and diligent of colonial peoples. Like the Puritans of New England, they had a body of doctrine that taught simplicity and sobriety, diligence and thrift. They too believed that it was sinful to waste anything, including time, and that it was wicked to be extravagant in anything, or to be ostentatious in dress. With these beliefs, they also achieved material success. Though they were not supposed to make a display of wealth, rich Quakers had to do something with their money; so they built great houses and filled them with comfortable furniture, simple but good. In time, prosperity made them relax, and some of the wealthier Quaker merchants of Philadelphia rode through the streets in fine coaches, as magnificent as any English lord's.

The Quakers were opposed to frivolity of all kinds and frowned on dancing and theatrical entertainments. Yet their opposition to gaiety was less stern than that of the Puritans and they were in general a gentler and more hospitable people. Travelers commented upon the beauty of Quaker girls whose simple dress enhanced rather than diminished their looks.

Since the Quakers were pacifists, they were opposed to war in all forms, even to fighting the Indians. Fortunately William Penn made a series of treaties with the Indians for the purchase of land, and both sides religiously kept these treaties. The French writer Voltaire observed that these were the only treaties not sealed with an oath—which Quakers refused to take—and the only treaties never broken.

Although fighting did erupt eventually on the frontiers of the colony, the Quakers by this time had a bulwark there of fighting Scottish Presbyterians. The Presbyterian Scots, who poured into Pennsylvania by the thousands in the eighteenth century, pushed on beyond the Germans to the distant frontiers where they seized such land as they wanted. They equated the Indians with the Amalekites of the Bible and found a text that justified slaying them and taking their land. They became the typical frontiersmen and were the spearhead of the push westward.

During the eighteenth century, as wealth increased in all of the colonies from Maine to Georgia, and as more tolerant ideas filtered into the people's thinking, particularly in the more urban regions, many of the old religious bans against games and innocent pleasures were forgotten or disregarded. Plays could be given even in Boston by the end of the colonial period. Tolerance of other religions was such that by the time of the Revolution, Catholics and Jews could worship without restrictions in all of the colonies, and in New York and Newport, Rhode Island, the Jews had synagogues. The Jewish synagogue in Newport, built by the first professional architect in America, Peter Harrison, was regarded as one of the most beautiful religious buildings in the colonies.

Religious fervor, which had diminished with the increase in luxuries, received a new stimulus as a result of a revival which swept through all of the English colonies and profoundly affected the religious attitudes in every region. This revival is known as the Great Awakening. It began about 1734 and continued for several years. One of its leaders was Jonathan Edwards, a Calvinist preacher of Northampton, Massachusetts, and another was George Whitefield, a disciple of John Wesley, whose followers became known as Methodists. No two men could have been more unlike, one a learned scholar and the other a fiery evangelist, yet they both helped to stir the people into an emotional frenzy.

Edwards was convinced that religious faith in New England had become stagnant and had lost its earlier fervor and zeal. In his preaching he set out to stir his congregations out of their lethargy. His most famous sermon, "Sinners in the Hands of an Angry God," preached in 1741, was calculated to frighten the wits out of indolent Christians and sinners. Choosing as his text, "Their foot shall slide in due time," he vividly impressed upon his hearers the imminence of their slide into a hell of burning sulphur and brimstone. Edwards soon had sinners weeping and wailing and throwing themselves upon the ground in an agony of repentance.

Whitefield's sermons had an even greater emotional impact upon his hearers, and his influence was more widespread than Edwards' because, from the time of his arrival

183

in Georgia in 1738, he traveled up and down the colonies preaching and exhorting sinners to repent. Whitefield had a cast in one eye that gave him a particularly hypnotic appearance when he turned upon a congregation already cringing from his eloquence and demanded that they give their hearts to God. They forthwith fell on their knees, or prostrated themselves upon the floor, weeping and asking forgiveness for sins real or imagined. David Garrick, the greatest English actor of the eighteenth century, who had heard Whitefield preach in England, declared that he would give a hundred guineas if he could say the word "Oh!" with the emotional effect that Whitefield achieved. And Benjamin Franklin, who once went to hear Whitefield determined to put nothing in the collection plate, was so moved that he emptied his pockets. Many other preachers besides Edwards and Whitefield took part in the Great Awakening, but these two were the most famous for their eloquence and for the emotional effect that they had on their congregations.

This emotional outpouring had several effects. Conservative folk in the Congregational and Presbyterian churches who objected to emotionalism deserted to the Anglican (Episcopal) Church which frowned on such behavior. The Baptists and the Methodists, who did not object to emotionalism, gained in numbers. The revival caused a split among the Presbyterians. The radical attitudes in religion also helped to spread radical ideas in politics. The type of religious revivalism displayed in the Great Awakening became characteristic of some of the less conventional sects in later periods. From this time onward, "camp meetings" with revivalistic preaching such as Whitefield had popularized were frequent in backwoods communities. They were often the occasion, not only of religious fervor, but of considerable merriment and love-making among the young people who flocked to these services. The emotional

184

outlet that they offered was not confined exclusively to religious feelings.

Although religious beliefs varied widely in the seventeenth and eighteenth centuries, from region to region and from decade to decade, religion was a powerful influence everywhere. Even so worldly a figure as William Byrd of Westover, Virginia, who was anything but a model of religious propriety, set an example by going to church regularly. He also read an incredible number of sermons, though with what benefit one is left to wonder. For instance, on Christmas night, 1710, he recorded in his *Diary*: "In the evening I read a sermon in Mr. Norris, but a quarrel which I had with my wife hindered my taking more notice of it."

William Byrd, reading sermons by candlelight in his Virginia library; Cotton Mather, diligently writing sermons for distribution throughout New England; Benjamin Franklin, out of curiosity attending a revival service preached by George Whitefield; people of all classes concerned about religious problems, some in fear of their souls, others concerned because religion was mixed with social and political affairs—this universal preoccupation with religion was characteristic of the colonial period.

8

Sports, Pastimes, and Holidays

Young people today have so much leisure and so many forms of amusement that they find it hard to imagine a period when everybody was so busy with the struggle for the raw essentials of life that there was no time for formal entertainment. Yet that was precisely the situation in the early days of colonial settlement. When men and women found themselves on the barren shores of a new country with a forest to conquer and hostile savages to repel, neither they nor their children could be much concerned with amusements and entertainment. They had enough to do to stay alive. But as soon as life became easier, as soon as towns were established, or plantations were laid out and houses built, the inhabitants began to seek diversions from the daily routine of existence. Early in their experience settlers in the new country found pleasure in certain of their labors and even devised some amusements. All work

The homes of the colonists were as barren of amusement within as the wilderness without. Toys were scarce even by 1800 when the Lippett farmhouse was built. One can hear the squabbles in this attic bedroom over whose turn it was to ride the rocking horse next. *Courtesy, The Farmers' Museum, New York State Historical Association, Cooperstown, N.Y. LeBel Studio photograph.*

and no play never made Jack a dull boy, for not even in the strictest New England or Quaker communities could the elders keep young people from a certain amount of play and gaiety. Nevertheless, opportunities for pleasure outside of one's work were scarce and nobody in North America had a surplus of leisure before the rise of our modern mechanical civilization.

Since Virginians, Carolinians, and Marylanders were less handicapped by religious restraints, as soon as they could find relief from the daily struggle against elemental nature, they began to enjoy certain sports and pastimes. Dancing was the most popular of the social activities in the southern colonies, and some form of dancing was enjoyed by all classes.

The great planters had stately ballrooms in their planta-

187

tion houses. There from time to time they held "assemblies" attended by the most beautiful girls from all the surrounding country. Young planters would ride for miles to attend these assemblies and would dance all night to music supplied sometimes by trained musicians but more often by white indentured servants whose skills had been discovered and developed, or, late in the period, by Negro fiddlers who had learned the art from white musicians.

So fond of dancing were the Virginians that they sometimes danced the whole night through and into the next day. On one occasion, late in the seventeenth century, the

Toys like these in a seventeenth-century Dutch toy stall occasionally trickled to or were imitated in the colonies. Hobbyhorses were the toy cars of the time, drums were of the militia, not bongo, variety, and dolls, as always, dressed in the latest fashion. *From the Folger Library copy of Jacob Cats,* Alle de Wercken *(1657–59).*

Women least of all knew the luxury of leisure. Unlike the lilies of the field, they toiled and spun and were never done. *From the Folger Library copy of Thomas Firmin,* Some Proposals for the Imployment of the Poor *(1681).*

daughter of the Reverend Thomas Teakle, a well-to-do minister of Accomac County, created a scandal by giving a dance on a Saturday night while her father was absent from home. The company, carried away with enthusiasm, danced until the very hour of church service the next day, which was more than even an Anglican parson could condone.

Women least of all knew the luxury of leisure. A common proverb ran, "Man works from sun to sun, but woman's work is never done." That was literally true. She was responsible for the care, clothing, and feeding of her family, whatever her social status. If she had servants, she had to direct them, see that they did their work properly, show them how to do certain things, look after them when they were ill, and maintain a watchful eye at all times. If she did not have servants, as was the case with most of the women in the early settlements, she had even less leisure, for she not only had to bear and care for children, but she had to cook and wash for the whole family without benefit of any labor-saving device; she not only had to make garments for all the family, including the menfolk, but she had to spin the thread and weave the yarn into the cloth for these garments. She also had to knit socks and stockings. Her hands could never be idle, and she could not even afford the luxury of nodding quietly in the chimney corner. If she did, some duty would be neglected. She did not have time to worry about amusements, though she did manage at times to find pleasure in such communal activities as quilting parties. Pleasure in the colonial period, both for women and men, frequently had to be found in some essential activity.

The very adventure of coming to a new land provided entertainment for some of the earliest settlers, because the zest for adventure was the lure that induced them to come. Though hunting and fishing were as essential to life as farming, nevertheless these activities were enjoyed. Even

Colonial appetites were hearty and there were no prepared mixes. Even sausage had to be made "from the ground up," as the woman appears to be doing here. *From the Folger Library copy of Jacob Cats,* Alle de Wercken *(1657–59).*

fighting Indians was not without its thrills for adventure-seekers, however grim a business it was to those who wanted to establish their homes in peace.

The nature of the settlements, the climate, and the occupations of the various regions all helped to determine the kind of amusements that our ancestors enjoyed. The warm weather of the South and the plantation life there gave greater opportunities for outdoor activities. The compact town life of New England made possible pleasure and amusements that could not be had on farms and plantations in rural localities. Religion also influenced amusements, as we have seen, and the gaieties of Charleston, Williamsburg, or Annapolis would have been frowned upon in Boston and even in Philadelphia until late in the eighteenth century.

But men, women, and children all required some diver-

"After breakfast we all retired into the dancing room . . . to step a minuet." Illustration on title page of John Playford's *The Dancing Master*, ca. 1725, which was probably used by colonial dancing masters. *From the Folger Library copy.*

sion from the routine of existence, and they all managed to find something to divert them whatever their region and their religion.

Dancing masters and musicians were common in Virginia, Maryland, and South Carolina from an early date. In 1716 the Board of Visitors of the College of William and Mary granted William Levingstone permission "to make use of the lower room at the south end of the College for teaching the scholars and others to dance until his

The music and instructions for performing Kemp's Jig, from John Playford's *The Dancing Master*. William Kemp was the comedian and dancer in Shakespeare's company, especially celebrated for his morris dance from London to Norwich in 1599. *From the Folger Library copy.*

own dancing school in Williamsburg be finished." Levingstone placed Charles and Mary Stagg in charge. After her husband's death, Mrs. Stagg organized and conducted "dancing assemblies" in Williamsburg.

So important was dancing in the education of Virginians that the Reverend Hugh Jones, a professor at the College of William and Mary, recommended that the College take a hand in providing training for its students. "As for the accomplishments of music, dancing, and fencing," he remarked, "they may be taught by such as the president and masters shall appoint at such certain times as they shall fix for those purposes."

To provide a place for assemblies, four prominent planters, Henry Corbin, Thomas Gerard, John Lee, and Isaac Allerton, in 1670 built a "banqueting house" to be used by each family in turn for the entertainment of wives, sweethearts, and friends. This jointly owned banqueting house was needed because the ballrooms in the houses of these planters were not large enough for all who attended.

Philip Fithian, a young Presbyterian minister from Princeton who came to Virginia in 1773 to serve as a tutor in the household of Robert Carter of Nomini Hall, at first regarded dancing as too worldly an amusement for a minister, but he soon came to regret his own inability to participate in the balls. He could see no evil in the graceful dances characteristic of that period and social class. In his *Diary* for December 18, 1773, he describes the visit of a dancing master, a certain Mr. Christian:

After breakfast we all retired into the dancing room, and after the scholars had their lesson singly round, Mr. Christian very politely requested me to step a minuet; I excused myself however but signified my peculiar pleasure in the accuracy of their performance. There were several minuets danced with great ease and propriety, after which the whole company joined in country-dances [square-dances] and it was indeed beautiful to admiration to see such a number of young persons, set off by dress to the best advantage, moving easily to the sound of

Horses in colonial days, like cars today, were a source of endless interest and diversion, as well as of transportation. Wealthy Virginians then as now were proud of their stables. *From the Folger Library copy of Diderot and D'Alembert,* Encyclopédie. Recueil des Planches *(1751–65).*

well-performed music and with perfect regularity. . . . When it was too dark to dance, the young gentlemen walked over to my room. We conversed till half after six. Nothing is now to be heard of in conversation but the balls, the foxhunts, the fine entertainments, and the good fellowship which are to be exhibited at the approaching Christmas. . . . When the candles were lighted we all repaired for the last time into the dancing room; first each couple danced a minuet; then all joined as before in the country dances; these continued till half after seven when Mr. Christian retired, and at the proposal of several (with Mr. Carter's approbation) we played "Button" to get pawns for redemption. Here I could join with them, and indeed it was carried on with sprightliness and decency. In the course of redeeming the pawns, I had several kisses of the ladies. . . . So soon as we rose after supper, the company formed into a semicircle round the fire, and Mr. Lee, by the voice of the company was chosen Pope, and Mr. Carter, Mr. Christian, Mrs. Carter, Mrs. Lee, and the rest of the company were appointed Friars in the play [game] called "Break the Pope's Neck." Here we had great diversion in the respective judgments upon offenders, but we were all dismissed by ten and retired to our several rooms.

This passage describing the visit of the dancing master to Nomini Hall and the games played by the guests and members of the household gives a picture of the characteristic entertainment at one of the great Virginia plantations in the eighteenth century. In addition to dances and games of the sort that Fithian mentions, card playing was also popular. Everybody from the visiting minister to the children of the family took part in some card game and normally played for some stake. William Byrd of Westover frequently mentions in his *Diary* that he played at cards and "lost my money." He apparently was an inveterate loser.

Wealthy planters with ballrooms and skilled musicians had no monopoly of dancing, for it was almost universally enjoyed. The Negro slaves in their quarters developed characteristic dances to the accompaniment of hand clapping or of a fiddle played by one of their number. In the back country, especially among Scottish settlers, dancing to fiddle tunes was especially popular. These were traditional Scottish dances that the settlers had brought with them, the jigs being the favorites. Occasionally a preacher would decide that dancing was leading the people astray and would preach against it—to no avail. Because the fiddle was invariably the instrument used at these dances, the preachers referred to it as "the devil's instrument."

In all of the southern colonies, horse racing was a favorite sport enjoyed by everyone. The rich planters were proud of their racing stables and they jealously guarded their privilege of entering horses in the races, though the whole

THE

Commendation

of Cockes, and Cock-fighting.

Wherein is shewed, that Cocke-
fighting *was before the com-
ming of* Christ.

LONDON,

Printed for *Henrie Tomes,* and are
to be sold at his Shop ouer a-
gainst Graies Inne gate in Holburne,
1607.

Cockfighting was a favorite sport of long "commendation," as
pointed out on this title page to *The Commendation of Cockes,*
printed in London in 1607. *From the Folger Library copy.*

countryside was welcome to come and enjoy the sight. A scandal was caused in York County, Virginia, in 1674 because one James Bullock, a tailor, was so presumptuous as to enter his horse in a race against a gentleman's horse. Betting on the horse races was usually heavy and many a planter lost more than he could afford. Gambling was one of the vices of the colonial South. All classes had a weakness for betting on anything from cards to horses.

Although horse racing was a particular addiction of the southern colonies, it was not confined to this region. New Englanders in the eighteenth century raced horses, with the excuse that it was a useful way of improving the breed. Rhode Island, which had plantations somewhat like those in the South, raised horses for export to the West Indies, and enjoyed racing them. Cockfighting was another sport that anyone with the inclination to breed gamecocks could enjoy, and cockfighting took place on all levels of society.

An Anglican parson in New York, the Reverend John Sharpe, kept a journal between the years 1710 and 1713 in which, among other things, he wrote down the times that he attended cockfights. Sometimes he went from his church service directly to the cockpits. Planters bred gamecocks and bet on their favorites as they did on their horses. Backwoods chicken-raisers also bred gamecocks and fought them for the entertainment of themselves and their neighbors. This sport has never completely died out and is still carried on surreptitiously in many rural areas even though in most jurisdictions it is now illegal.

Hunting and fishing were universal sports throughout the colonies, though the type of hunting varied with the nature of the game and the customs of the region. Foxes were at first regarded as vermin and were killed as were other pests. Not until late in the eighteenth century did fox hunting in the English manner become a fashionable sport in Virginia and in Maryland. Since deer were prized for food and for their skins, deer hunting everywhere from the ear-

liest times was a sport that every boy and man enjoyed.
Boys learned to shoot at an early age, and the highest
ambition of almost every boy was to own a gun of his own.

In seventeenth-century New England wolves were a
menace and a bounty was offered for wolf heads. Men and
boys in the time that they could spare from routine tasks
hunted wolves and brought in their heads to the magistrates
of the townships. It was the custom in many districts to
hang wolf heads against the outside walls of the meetinghouse.

Fishing, like deer hunting, was a useful sport, for fish
were a valuable food in all areas. Furthermore it was the
most democratic of all sports, for fancy and expensive fishing tackle had not yet been invented, and anybody with a
cane pole, a line, and a hook could enjoy an hour or two
on the bank of some stream.

Besides fishing with hook and line, seining with nets was
an activity that provided not only profit from the huge

The cockpits, like horse racing, provided an outlet for the gambling
instinct that had brought many colonists to the New World in the
first place. *From the Folger Library copy of Charles Cotton,* The
Complete Gamester *(1680).*

Hunting, fishing and falconry in Virginia in the early seventeenth century, as pictured in Theodor de Bry's *America*, Part X, published in 1619. *From the Folger Library copy.*

catches of fish but a great deal of fun for the boys and young men who took part. During the runs of herring in the New England rivers, however, the great loads of fish scooped from the streams must have been more labor than sport. In the South, seining was a sport that even gentlemen-planters enjoyed. John Harrower, an indentured white servant of Colonel William Daingerfield's of Fredericksburg, Virginia, tells in his *Journal* for April 22, 1775, of such fishing:

At three p.m. went to New Post where the Colonel and several gentlemen had been all day hauling a seine net and had catched a good deal [of] herrings and white fish; but at noon their net got foul of some driven tree at bottom and continued so until I went off in a canoe and got it cleared.

199

Harrower, who had been brought over as a schoolmaster, was invited from time to time to go fishing with Colonel Daingerfield. An entry in his *Journal* for June 11, 1774, reads:

At nine a.m. left school and went afishing on the river with the Colonel, his eldest [son], and another gentleman in two canoes. Mrs. Daingerfield, another lady, and the other two boys met us at Snow Creek in the chair [two-wheeled buggy] at two p.m. when we all dined on fish under a tree.

Such fishing picnics were frequent with all classes.

Since fish and game abounded in all the colonies and the woods and streams were free of any restrictions, these outdoor sports were available to everyone. Even a boy unable to own a gun could trap and snare animals, or track them to their dens in the snow. Rabbit hunting, when the rabbits could not run fast enough in soft snow to escape, was regarded as great fun. Hunting and fishing, so important in the economic life of early America, became traditional sports that have endured in popularity to the present time. Only the destruction of forests and the closing of open land has diminished hunting as a universal sport. Even though many streams have been ruined by pollution, fishing continues to be one of our favorite outdoor activities.

Although the stricter Puritans in New England did their best to keep young people from wasting their time in amusements of any kind, they were unable, with all of their warnings, fines, and punishments, to suppress youthful human nature, and young New Englanders gradually came to enjoy as many sports and pastimes as were common in the less rigid colonies. Despite the railings of the preachers, dancing was a common form of entertainment in New England from the late seventeenth century onward. The Governor of Massachusetts gave a great ball in Boston in 1713, to the scandal of some of the ministers, and the guests danced till three o'clock in the morning. Elsewhere in New England, dancing was enjoyed as much

The method of exterminating foxes before fox hunting with horse and hound came into fashion. *From the Folger Library copy of Leonard Mascall,* A Booke of Fishing with Hooke and Line *(1590).*

as it was in the South, though dancing teachers were some-times harassed by the magistrates and refused the use of rooms for their schools.

Town life made possible some sports that could not be carried on in the sparsely settled regions. Football and stoolball were played on the town commons. The latter was a kind of croquet in which a ball was knocked from wicket to wicket. Football was a rough-and-tumble scrim-mage without the elaborate rules that we know today. One side, with any number of players, lined up against another and tried to push a ball through to the opposite side. Heads were bashed and noses bloodied and the game sometimes degenerated into a free-for-all fight. This type of football had been played in England for generations and is sup-posed to have originated in primitive times, when opposing sides would fight for the head of the victim of a human sacrifice. At any rate, English writers of books of conduct, as well as New England preachers, condemned football as dangerous and liable to break the limbs and necks of the players.

Card playing was not uncommon in New England, though it too was frowned on by the clergy and in some areas forbidden. Some towns made the sale of playing cards illegal, but that did not stop their circulation. A custom developed of writing invitations to balls on the backs of playing cards, a practice which gave the preachers an even greater abhorrence of these items, which they called the "devil's picture books." Billiards were played here and there in all of the colonies. A public house in Charlestown advertised in the *New England Courant* for April 30, 1722, that gentlemen could find recreation there with a game of billiards. William Byrd of Virginia owned a bil-liard table, as did many others.

Two sports impossible in the South found great favor in New York and spread to New England. They were sleigh riding and ice skating. The Dutch who first settled New

Fishing was the universal sport. Boys could come home from a day's escape on the "crick" full of virtue—if their baskets were full of fish. *From the Folger Library copy of Francis Barlow,* A Sett of Prints *(ca. 1671).*

York introduced the sleigh and the ice skate, and both became popular in the eighteenth century wherever the climate favored such activities. Madame Sarah Knight, who made an overland journey from Boston to New York in 1704 and kept a famous diary of her trip, reported on the sport of sleigh riding there:

Their diversions in the winter is [*sic*] riding sleighs about three or four miles out of town where they have houses of entertainment at a place called the Bowery, and some go to friends' houses who handsomely treat them. Mr. Burroughs carried his spouse and daughter and myself out to one Madame Dowes, a gentlewoman that lived at a farmhouse, who gave us a handsome entertainment of five or six dishes and choice beer and metheglin, cider, etc., all which she said was the produce of her farm. I believe we met 50 or 60 sleighs that day. They fly with great swiftness and some are so furious that they'll turn out of the path for none except a loaden cart. Nor do they

Rabbit hunting without guns. *From the Folger Library copy of Francis Barlow,* A Sett of Prints *(ca. 1671).*

spare for any diversion the place affords, and sociable to a degree, their tables being as free to their neighbors as to themselves.

By the end of the colonial period and long afterward, sleigh rides—both by day and by moonlight—were events to which young people particularly looked forward with delight and anticipation.

Madame Knight's description of the hospitality in New York indicates one of the traditional characteristics of that city's entertainment. From the earliest times, it was famous for its food and drink. Indeed, reformers complained that taverns far outnumbered churches, and that the inhabitants were given to drunkenness and gluttony. Since New York under the Dutch and later under English governors was free from Puritan influences, it had none of the restraints that applied in New England and it was natural that worldly pleasures should prevail. Players were welcomed to New

York and it had a theater long before theatrical entertainment was legal in any New England city.

In spite of the hard work required to settle the wilderness, all the colonies took time to celebrate occasional holidays. Although the New England Puritans and the Quakers were desperately afraid of wasting time, even they had to take a few days off during the year to observe special occasions. The feast days of the Anglican Church were religiously disregarded by the New England Puritans but they gradually added special days of their own: Election Days, Training (or Muster) Days, and days set apart for thanksgiving and for fasting. Contrary to general opinion, Thanksgiving Day was not a regularly fixed day until modern times, though various colonies proclaimed a day of thanksgiving whenever it suited them. Sometimes more than one day of thanksgiving was observed with feasting and good cheer; occasionally the day of feasting was followed by a day of fasting—a not unwise provision.

The precise date of the first Thanksgiving Day, that proclaimed by the Pilgrims at Plymouth sometime in the autumn of 1621, is not known. In a letter dated December 11, 1621, Edward Winslow wrote to a friend in England describing the event that has become so important in American folklore:

Our harvest being gotten in, our Governor [William Bradford] sent four men on fowling that so we might after a more special manner rejoice together after we had gathered the fruit of our labors. They four in one day killed so much fowl as, with a little help beside, served the company almost a week. At which time, amongst other recreations, we exercised our arms, many of the Indians coming amongst us, and amongst the rest their greatest king, Massasoit, with some 90 men, whom for three days we entertained and feasted. And they went out and killed five deer which they brought to the plantation and bestowed on our Governor and upon the Captain [Miles Standish] and others.

Governor Bradford in his history *Of Plymouth Plantation* reported that "besides waterfowl there was great store of

Not the least of the pleasures of hunting was the roaring fire at day's end and eating the "bag." Here fresh game hangs from game hooks in the kitchen of Raleigh Tavern, famous eighteenth-century Williamsburg hostelry. *Courtesy, Colonial Williamsburg, Williamsburg, Va. Thomas L. Williams photograph.*

wild turkeys, of which they took many, besides venison, etc. Besides they had about a peck of meal a week to a person, or now since harvest, Indian corn to that proportion." This first Thanksgiving, as we can see, went on for three days and was the occasion for feasting and for impressing the Indians with the military prowess of Captain Miles Standish's little troop.

In the Massachusetts Bay Colony, Commencement Day at Harvard became one of the most important holidays of the year. After the sermons and the exercises, the day was given over to feasting and jollification. Beginning about 1730, Commencement Day was set on Friday so that there would be "less remaining time in the week to be spent in frolicking," as one president of the college explained. Election Day was another time of festivity in all of the New England colonies. Despite the sermons of the preachers, the day quickly took on a distinctly unreligious tone. One minister complained that it had become an occasion when men gathered "to smoke, carouse, and swagger, and dishonor God with greater bravery." In some communities, a special beer was brewed for the occasion. In others, it was the custom for housewives to bake a particular kind of election cake.

Even more boisterous than Election Day, in all of the colonies, was Training, or Muster, Day. A frontier society had to maintain a militia ready to repel attacks from Indians or marauders from the sea. At intervals, the militia, composed of all able-bodied citizens of a certain age, had to be called together for drills. The amount of training was negligible. After going through the manual of arms, marching up and down the town common or the village green, and firing their muskets a time or two, the formal muster

Bowling was a popular game with all ages then as now. There was more leisure in late sixteenth-century Europe than in the new colonies, as this garden scene indicates. *From the Folger Library copy of* Le Centre de l'Amour *(ca. 1600).*

was over, but the celebrating had just begun. Contests of marksmanship were usual on these occasions, and prizes were offered for the best shots. The targets might be live turkeys or ducks, for our ancestors were not squeamish. Before the day was over the participants had consumed vast quantities of beer and rum and engaged in more than one impromptu wrestling match and fist fight. If some of the crowd reeled home with broken heads and black eyes, that did not decrease the pleasure of the others. Muster Day was an occasion that no boy wanted to miss.

Madame Knight, describing the holidays in Connecticut, remarked:

Their diversions in this part of the country are on lecture days and training days mostly. On the former there is riding from town to town. And on training days the youth divert themselves by shooting at the target, as they call it (but it much resembles a pillory), where he that hits nearest the white has some yards of red ribbon presented him, which being tied to his hatband, the two ends streaming down his back, he is led away in triumph with great applause as the winners of the Olympic Games.

Shrove Tuesday, which had a long tradition of boisterous celebration in England, was observed in some localities with similar outbursts on the part of apprentices and other unruly youths. Judge Sewall of Boston complained in his *Diary* for February 15, 1687, about the ancient custom of "cock-skailing" on Shrove Tuesday: "Jos. Maylem carries a cock at his back, with a bell in his hand, in the Main Street; several follow him blindfold, and under pretence of striking him or his cock, with great cart-whips strike passengers, and make great disturbance."

Another holiday that lent itself to boisterous misbehavior was November 5, Guy Fawkes Day. Guy Fawkes was the leader of a Catholic conspiracy that, in the reign of King James I, had plotted to blow up the English Houses of Parliament. The discovery of the Gunpowder Plot in the nick of time has been commemorated in England ever

208

since. In the colonies the anniversary provided an opportunity for young people to organize parades with an effigy of Guy Fawkes, or of the Pope, which they carried through the streets and then burned on a great bonfire. In some Puritan communities Guy Fawkes Day was called Pope's Day, a term later corrupted in Newcastle, New Hampshire, to "Pork Night." The rowdiness of this celebration in some parts of New England became such a nuisance that the authorities tried to suppress it.

New York had a holiday peculiar to it called Pinkster Day, derived from the Dutch word for Pentecost. On that

Ice skating was a popular, and entertaining, winter sport introduced by the Dutch in New Amsterdam. *From the Folger Library copy of Jacob Cats,* Alle de Wercken *(1657–59).*

A convivial stag party which supposedly took place about 1760 at Steepbrook, one of Peter Manigault's rice plantations near Charleston. The dialogue spoken by the gentlemen is as follows:

1. PETER MANIGAULT — Your Tost [*sic*] Howarth
2. TAYLOR, AN OFFICER — Hey to the Midnight—Hark-a-way, Hark-a-way
3. DEMARE, AN OFFICER — Success to Caroline G-d dame
4. CAPTAIN MASSEY — This one bumper, dear Isaac
5. ISAAC CODIN — I shall be Drunk, I tell ye, Major
6. COYTMORE, AN OFFICER — Whose tost is it
7. COL. ROBERT HOWARTH — Squire Isaac, your wig, you Dog
8. GEORGE ROUPELL — Pray less noise Gentn

From George Roupell's drawing, "Mr. Peter Manigault and his Friends." Courtesy, The Henry Francis du Pont Winterthur Museum, Winterthur, Del.

day, by tradition, Negro slaves in New York had license to hold a rousing celebration with drums and dancing in the streets. The Pinkster Day festivities of the slaves at Albany were particularly exciting, with parades in costume and dancing.

The observance of Christmas, which was frowned upon by the Puritans as a relic of superstitition from the time when the church was Catholic, had far less emphasis anywhere in the colonies than it has today. William Byrd of Virginia mentions no special celebrations of the day beyond the entertainment of guests at Westover and attendance at church. John Harrower, the indentured servant-schoolmaster of Colonel William Daingerfield of Fredericksburg, noted in his *Journal* no special Christmas celebration. For December 25, 1774, he reports: "Christmas Day, stayed at home all day along with the overseer and children because I had no saddle to go to church with. In the morning the Colonel ordered up to school two bottles of the best rum and sugar for me." The rum must have got a hold on Harrower, for on Christmas Day a year later he simply reports, "At night, drunk," and on the next day, "Sick all day, at night ditto." Philip Fithian reported of the observance of Christmas at Nomini Hall that he was wakened by the firing of guns, which was customary on that day. This noisy custom has persisted in the South, where firecrackers are more usual at Christmas than on the Fourth of July.

As a few towns grew into cities in the eighteenth century—Boston, New York, Newport, Philadelphia, and Charleston—entertainment and amusements became more sophisticated. By the end of the colonial period, all of these cities had some form of theatrical entertainment and some had regular concerts by professional musicians. New York and Charleston gave the most encouragement to stage players and both had thriving theaters. The performance of plays by amateurs was not uncommon and offered pleasant

211

diversion to stage-struck young people. Music and singing teachers were in great demand in all of the colonies and music had an important place in many households. Charleston, South Carolina, probably had more musicians than any other city in proportion to its population; in 1762 it organized the Saint Cecilia Society, the oldest musical society in America. This society maintained an orchestra of paid musicians which gave regular concerts, and it sponsored performances by amateur musicians of the city. In all of the principal cities groups of singers and instrumentalists met to sing and play together for their own enjoyment.

Colonial people, wherever they lived, had fewer amusements that they could buy than even the most deprived person has today: no moving picture, no radio, no television, no comic strip, no cheap paperback book, no amusement park, no automobile, no social service to organize entertainment, no belief anywhere that something must be done to help people utilize their leisure. Such entertainment as people had, young or old, they had to de-

The stocks were a simple, inexpensive, and effective means of dealing with the myriad minor offenses the Puritan preachers railed against. They may, perhaps, be considered symbolic of the many strictures, economic as well as religious, upon life in the colonial period. *From the Folger Library copy of Thomas Harman,* A Caveat . . . for Commen Cursetors *(1567).*

Children's games were much the same everywhere in the colonial period and many have persisted with little change to the present day. In this seventeenth-century illustration, the swing, stilts, top, and tenpins look surprisingly familiar. *From the Folger Library copy of J. A. Comenius,* Orbis Sensualium Pictus *(1685).*

vise for themselves. Their amusements came from participation, not from looking on. Spectator sports, except for horse racing, cockfighting, and a few similar activities, were almost nonexistent. To find enjoyment, one had to take part in something. This necessity trained our ancestors to develop their own inner resources.

Reading provided enjoyment for many people, and colonial households were not without books. A library might consist of only a handful of books, but these were carefully chosen and carefully read, for both entertainment and instruction. If a house was so destitute of books that it contained only the Bible, the chances are that it was read and re-read. A few books well read provided more mental training and stimulus, and sometimes more genuine satisfactions, than many books skimmed through without appreciation.

One of the most important of all forms of diversion in the colonial period was the simplest: the sheer pleasure that people obtained from one another's company. Family conclaves, neighborhood gatherings, picnics, church socials, visits with friends and acquaintances—all of these means of social communication that are now overshadowed by mechanical devices—played a far more important role in colonial life than they do today.

The family was a social unit of great importance, for the family stayed together for work and play in a way that is unknown now. In a period when there were no labor-

In the long winter evenings, families gathered about the kitchen table or hearth for storytelling or reading aloud. The inevitable rifle and full powder horn over the mantel added real shivers to Indian tales. *Courtesy, The Henry Francis du Pont Winterthur Museum, Winterthur, Del. Photograph by Gilbert Ask.*

saving devices, mutual helpfulness was essential. When the daily chores were done, few external diversions lured the family to go its separate ways, as is our custom. The family not only had to work together but had to find amusements in which all could join. In the evening they might gather to hear someone read aloud, or they might listen to their elders telling stories. Storytelling had been a popular diversion from the most distant past and it continued to have its place until radio and television made it virtually extinct. The family might sing together or play games.

The church was another institution significant for the sheer entertainment that it provided. When we contemplate the misery of sitting through two-hour sermons in the arctic cold of a Puritan meetinghouse in the winter, we can see little except punishment in that ordeal, but actually that was only one aspect of the case. In all of the colonies, whatever their religion, the church provided a meeting place where neighbors and friends met together for conversation, gossip, and perhaps a sly horse trade to be consummated on the morrow. The country church in particular served as the unifying influence in each community. Church picnics, church socials, church recitations, even lectures and sometimes the sermons themselves provided entertainment and stimulation.

In an era when many families lived in isolated areas, hospitality was dispensed more freely than now, for a guest meant a break in the routine of ordinary life and was doubly welcome, even though he might be only a peddler or some nondescript wayfarer. The exception to this rule was found in some New England towns, which looked askance at traveling strangers who might settle down and become a charge of the community. But travelers in the southern colonies were certain to find a bed and a meal at any planter's house. European observers commented that one could travel across the whole of the southern colonies without ever paying for a room or a meal.

Convivial gatherings of various sorts added to the pleasures of life everywhere. The tavern was the poor man's club. Here anyone could sit and smoke his pipe, drink his pint of beer, and exchange news and gossip. After a long day's work, a couple of hours spent in the village tavern lifted a man's spirit though it might drain his pocket of his last penny. Reforming preachers sometimes railed at the waste of time and money in these "dens of iniquity," but their words kept few men away from the warm fire and the cheering drink. By the approach of the Revolution, the taverns were important centers of discussion, where the tyranny of King George was nightly damned.

Busy as were colonial Americans, they managed to find time for pleasure and for social communication on whatever level they found themselves. Great merchants in Boston, New York, Philadelphia, or Charleston met in their clubs and coffeehouses; village cobblers and blacksmiths swapped a little tobacco at the local tavern and drank their beer as they talked of high taxes, hard times, or the glorious future of their country. Work was hard in colonial America but men and women all found some means of amusement and of entertaining themselves. Nobody ever felt sorry for himself because there was nothing to do.

9

Military Adventures and Settlement in the West

From the time the first settlers landed at Jamestown until the Peace of Paris in 1763, the English colonists held a precarious position on the Atlantic coastline, with a vast interior occupied by hostile Indians. Traditional enemies, France and Spain, held territories to the north and south of them. A great danger lay in the possibility that France and Spain would cut them off from expansion inland, as these two powers swept in a great arc behind them. The French occupied Canada, including the Valley of the St. Lawrence and the Great Lakes region. They were poised to sweep down the Ohio and Mississippi river systems. The Spaniards who held Mexico and Florida were ready to attack Georgia and encircle the southern colonies from the rear. Both the Spaniards and the French had Indian allies who, from time to time, fell on outlying English settlements, slaughtered men, women, and children, and burned their cabins.

Cannon defending the early settlement of St. George Town, Bermuda. According to Captain John Smith, the town was named for Sir George Somers, admiral of the fleet that was dispersed by a hurricane in the West Indies in 1609. The wreck of Somers' flagship on one of the Bermuda islands provided the background for Shakespeare's *The Tempest*. The stocks defend the peace from within as the cannon from without. *From the 1631 edition of John Smith,* Generall Historie of Virginia *in the Folger Library*.

With this ever-present threat hanging over the English colonists, it was natural for them to think of self-defense and for every man to prepare as best he could to fight when necessary. From the beginning, Americans were frontiersmen standing on a border that they would have to defend and that they wanted to extend.

Every American boy learned as a matter of course to bear arms, to shoot with accuracy, and to drill with the militia. In all of the colonies, this citizen army, composed of every able-bodied man not too old or too young, stood ready to fight in defense of hearth and home. The ability and courage of these citizen soldiers was tried on more than one occasion and gave rise to the feeling that one American soldier was worth several of any other nationality, a feeling of overconfidence that sometimes proved a liability.

Intermittent war with the Indians on all the colonial borders was inevitable, for white men encroached on the Indians' hunting grounds and disturbed the game upon which the Indians depended for their sustenance. It was natural for the Indians to resist and to take the kind of vengeance that they were accustomed to take against intruders of their own race. The slaughter of white settlers, however, inflamed the feelings of survivors, who in turn wreaked their own revenge. Sporadic wars with the Indians in all border areas except, for a time, in Pennsylvania, became the normal mode of life. Since the Indians were often involved in intertribal fighting, the white men were sometimes able to pit one tribe against another. Not infrequently the settlers went to war with Indian allies.

The push of Puritan settlers into the Connecticut Valley angered the Pequot tribe, who murdered some of the interlopers. In 1637, an expedition surrounded over 500 Pequots in a hastily made fort at Mystic, which the colonists burned with most of its occupants. The ruthlessness of this slaughter of Indians is described by William Bradford in his history, *Of Plymouth Plantation*:

They [the English with their Indian allies, the Narragansetts] approached the same [the Pequot fort at Mystic] with great silence and surrounded it both with English and Indians, that they might not break out, and so assaulted them with great courage, shooting amongst them, and entered the fort with all speed. And those that first entered found sharp resistance from the enemy who both shot at and grappled with them; others ran into their houses and brought out fire and set them on fire, which soon took in their mat; and standing close together, with the wind all was quickly on a flame, and thereby more were burnt to death than was otherwise slain. It burnt their bowstrings and made them unserviceable. Those that escaped the fire were slain with the sword, some hewed to pieces, others run through with their rapiers, so as they were quickly des-

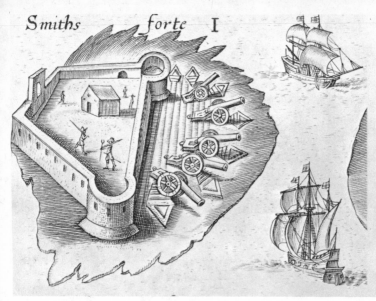

Evidence of the precarious position of early English colonists in the New World. Smith and Warwick forts were links in an elaborate chain of fortifications protecting St. George Town, Bermuda, and its approaches. As the ships indicate, Smith's Fort guarded the harbor channel. *From the Folger Library copy of John Smith,* Generall Historie of Virginia *(1631).*

patched and very few escaped. It was conceived they thus destroyed about 400 at this time. It was a fearful sight to see them thus frying in the fire and the streams of blood quenching the same, and horrible was the stink and scent thereof. But the victory seemed a sweet sacrifice, and they gave the praise to God, who had wrought so wonderfully for them, thus to enclose their enemies in their hands and give them so speedy a victory over so proud and insulting an enemy.

A later Indian war in New England, called King Philip's War after the Indian chief of the Wampanoag tribe known as King Philip, also resulted from the white man's greed for Indian land. It lasted for three years, from 1675 to 1678, and before it was over the Indians had killed one man in sixteen throughout New England and had burned

Wilderness fortifications were patterned on the latest European practices as promulgated by books like Peter Whithorne's *Certain Ways for the Ordering of Soldiers in Battle Array . . . and Also Figures of Certain New Plattes* [plans] *for Fortification of Towns*, 1562. Italian engineers were responsible for this fortification concept developed to accommodate the new artillery. A similarly designed wall survives around the town of Lucca, Italy, today. *From the Folger Library copy.*

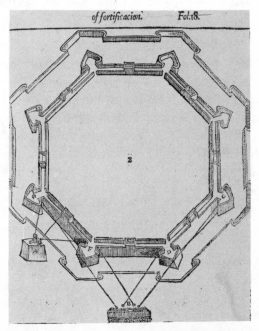

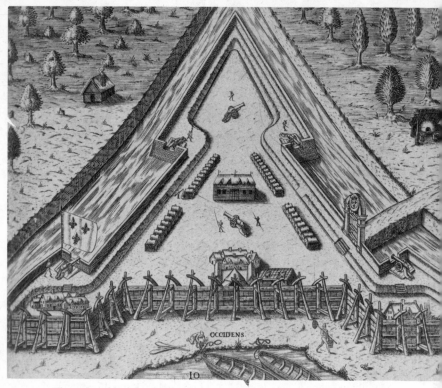

OCCIDENS.

The placement of artillery to defend the walls is shown in this contemporary engraving of the early French Fort Caroline in Florida. The first fort at Jamestown, as described by Master George Percy in 1607, "was triangle wise, having three Bulwarkes at every corner, like a halfe Moone, and foure or five pieces of Artillerie mounted in them." *From the Folger Library copy of Theodor de Bry,* America, *Part II (1591).*

twenty towns in Massachusetts and Connecticut. Massachusetts required every man between the ages of sixteen and sixty to serve in the militia. It also made death the penalty for evading military service. Indian fighting in these times was a grim and bitter business, a struggle for survival between two races who could find no practicable method of peaceful coexistence.

Some efforts, it is true, were made in all of the colonies to Christianize the Indians, but the results were not encouraging. The Virginians, though discouraged by Indian

Musketeer of the early colonial period as pictured in a contemporary manual of arms. *From the Folger Library copy of Jacob de Gheyn,* Maniement d'Armes *(1608).*

massacres in 1622 and 1644, provided for some education of the Indians when the College of William and Mary was founded in 1693. In New England, Harvard College had a few Indian students, but they did not turn out well. The most successful missionary effort was made in Massachusetts by the Reverend John Eliot, the "Apostle to the Indians," who translated the Bible into the dialect of the Algonquin language spoken by the Massachusetts Indians. Some of Eliot's "praying Indians," as the converts were called, were induced to settle near white communities where they could be kept from contamination by their savage brethren. The few Indians who were converted to Christianity, however, had no influence upon those who continued to endanger the frontiers.

The French were more successful than the English in making alliances with the Indians; in all the eighteenth-century wars, France's redskin allies were a great threat to the English colonists in the hinterland. War parties would swoop down from the woods and burn towns and villages after slaughtering the inhabitants. One of the worst massacres occurred at Deerfield, Massachusetts, in 1704, when a party of French and Indians attacked the village in the night. Fifty-three persons were killed and one hundred and eleven were taken prisoner and carried off by the attackers. A mound in the village graveyard at Deerfield, where the victims were buried in a common grave, can still be seen.

The colonists all feared the French, who incited their Indian allies to attack the English, but the feeling was strongest in New England and Virginia because both regions had borders exposed to French and Indian attack. At that time Virginia under its original grant claimed territory straight across the continent to the "Great South Sea," as the Pacific was called, and nobody knew how far away that might be. Land speculators were interested in Virginia's western territory across the mountains in the Ohio

Why regular drill of the militia was necessary. The sixteen steps illustrated show only half the operations involved in firing and reloading a musket. *From the Folger Library copy of Henry Hexham,* The Principles of the Art Military *(1637).*

Valley. Unhappily, France also claimed that territory, which made the region a scene of conflict.

The New Englanders were so concerned about the French and Indian onslaughts from Canada that they made a strenuous effort, during the War of the Austrian Succession in the 1740's, to neutralize that danger. The French had built a great fortress at Louisbourg on Cape Breton Island. In time of war, ships from this fortified port preyed on the New England fishing fleet and raided the coast. Because Louisbourg was such a continuing nuisance to them, New Englanders, with more enthusiasm than usual, joined with British forces in 1744 to destroy it. Farmers and fishermen from all over New England made up the militia army that marched against Louisbourg. They were commanded by William Pepperrell, a wealthy fish and lumber merchant from Kittery, Maine. To support this ragtag army, which brought along whatever military equipment they could gather together, the British sent a naval squadron from the West Indies. The army was in such high spirits, bolstered at times with copious supplies of rum, that one participant said its boisterousness reminded him of commencement day at Harvard. Nevertheless, the army, with the navy's help, maintained the siege of Louisbourg for forty-nine days and finally forced its surrender. The colonials were beside themselves with joy; and the authorities in London were so impressed with the fish merchant's prowess as a military commander that they had him made a baronet, the first American-born colonial to achieve nobility. The joy of the victors was doomed to disappointment, for, by the irony of imperial politics, England decided to give Louisbourg back to France in exchange for Madras, a city in India which the French had taken from the East India Company.

While the northern half of the colonies watched the French and Indians on their borders, the Virginians and Pennsylvanians were concerned about the incursions of the

226

same enemies in what they regarded as their own back country. In the effort to keep peace with the Indians, the Quaker government in Philadelphia did not encourage Pennsylvania settlers to push into the more distant Indian territories. But despite this hesitation on the part of the peace-loving Quakers, the Scottish immigrants moved into what was then the wild west and fought with Indians when they found it necessary.

Virginians were far less hesitant than the Pennsylvania Quakers about invading Indian territory. They managed to make a treaty with the Iroquois at a powwow held at Lancaster, Pennsylvania, in 1744, by which these Indians

"Those that escaped the fire were slain with the sword." All the massacres were not committed by Indians. *From the Folger Library copy of Theodor de Bry,* America, *Part IV (1594).*

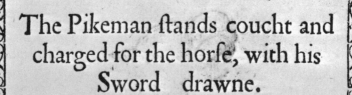

The Pikeman ſtands coucht and charged for the horſe, with his Sword drawne.

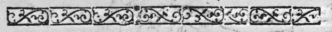

This Portraiture of charging for horſe, is to ſhew, that the Bow is very materiall for this ſeruice; for the fiue or ſixe firſt rankes ſtanding coucht at this charge, the middle and the reare may ſhoot their volleyes of arrowes, and therewith both gaule, wound, diſorder, and kill the enemy, both man and horſe.

The words of command are,

Fiue firſt Rankes draw your Swords cloſe to your pouldrons.

Charge at the foot, and couch low.

Middle and Reare, port and come up to your order, and ſhoot your Arrowes.

A pikeman in action. Pike and sword were important weapons in early colonial days, more reliable than muskets, especially in scantily trained hands. *From the Folger Library copy of William Neade,* The Double-Armed Man *(1625).*

ceded to Virginia territory of subject tribes in what is now western Pennsylvania. Land speculators in Virginia formed the Ohio Company, an organization designed to exploit western lands in the Ohio Valley and to trade with the Indians.

This company established a trading post at the present site of Cumberland, Maryland, and sent a famous scout and explorer, Christopher Gist, to spy out the hinterland. Gist crossed the Ohio at the site of Pittsburgh and made maps of parts of Ohio, Kentucky, and western Virginia. Several years later Gist was sent on a mission to the Cherokees in east Tennessee to try to enlist Indian allies there.

The French, meanwhile, had been developing their fur trade with the Indians in this western country. One of the chief items of trade was brandy, for which the Indians had developed a great appetite. They also supplied the Indians with guns and ammunition. Although most Indians preferred the kind of blankets that English traders offered, they liked brandy better than English rum, and English traders often found themselves outwitted by Frenchmen who showed greater skill in adapting their wares to Indian tastes.

By the 1750's Frenchmen were pushing down the Ohio River, and in 1752 a military expedition sent out by the Governor of Canada destroyed an English outpost on the Ohio. The next year the French took another English post on the Allegheny River.

Virginia traders brought news of all this back to Williamsburg. Concern over the western lands caused Governor Robert Dinwiddie in 1753 to send young Major George Washington to remonstrate with the French commander on the Ohio. The French blandly ignored Washington's demand that they withdraw from territory claimed by Virginia, and Dinwiddie sent another expedition with armed men to fortify the forks of the Ohio River. The French drove the Virginians out and built a fort of their own which they named Fort Duquesne, after the Governor of Canada. Eventually Fort Duquesne became Pittsburgh.

Since this invasion of the French threatened to take land that Virginia speculators hoped would make them rich, the Virginia government determined to take stronger action. The Governor sent Washington back with a force of militia to drive out the French. Meeting the enemy a few miles west of Great Meadows (near Uniontown, Pennsylvania), Washington opened fire and killed twenty men and the French commander. Though Washington was not aware of it, this was the first shot fired in what would become in a few years a final conflict with the French. The enraged French commander at Fort Duquesne sent a strong detachment which forced Washington to surrender his hastily fortified camp, Fort Necessity. Washington and his militia

Artillerymen of the Colonial Williamsburg Militia Company firing two French and Indian War cannons. The "uniforms" are those of eighteenth-century citizen soldiers. *Courtesy, Colonial Williamsburg, Williamsburg, Va.*

were permitted to keep their arms, provided they would promise to march back home and give no further trouble. This they had to do.

To help protect the colonial frontier against the French and Indians, the British government sent a professional soldier, General James Braddock, with two regiments of regulars to Virginia in 1755. Learning of young Washington's knowledge of the frontier, he added him to his staff. Setting out from Virginia with his redcoats and a body of colonial militia, Braddock marched on Fort Duquesne. His own troops knew nothing about backwoods fighting or Indian tactics. They had been drilled to fight on the open fields of Europe. The militia was poorly disciplined and had more rum to drink than was good for them. On July 9, 1755, the Braddock expedition had reached the Monongahela River, not far from their objective, when the French with their Indian allies fell upon them. Although the regulars knew how to form hollow squares and to fire their muskets in volleys, their tactics were ineffective against Indians skulking behind trees and Frenchmen already trained in forest warfare. Braddock, a brave but obstinate man, fell mortally wounded. Washington and the colonial officers did what they could to rally their men and to save the remnants of the army. Nevertheless, the encounter was a defeat and a disaster for the British and colonials. The survivors crept home, humiliated and discouraged. But the battle had proved one point, which future British commanders remembered. To fight Indians in the forests, one had to fight their way. A later commander, General John Forbes, remembered the lesson of Braddock's defeat and successfully occupied Fort Duquesne in November, 1758. After that it was named Fort Pitt, after William Pitt, the British Prime Minister.

War soon flamed along the whole frontier from Maine to Georgia. Virginia alone had more than three hundred miles of border exposed to attack. In the emergency, Gov-

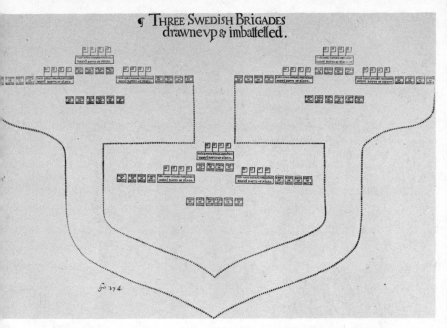

The very latest concept of battle deployment in Miles Standish's time. This diagram is from William Barriffe's *Military Discipline, or, The Young Artilleryman*, first published in 1635, a book that colonial settlers brought over to help them defend themselves against the savages. Unfortunately, the Indians had not studied the same book. *From the Folger Library copy of the second edition, 1639.*

ernor Dinwiddie made Washington, who was then only twenty-three years old, commander of the militia. Washington had the responsibility of protecting the settlers in the distant clearings from slaughter by the Indians and the marauding French, a task that his troops were too few to accomplish. He rarely had more than fifteen hundred men available for service. Though they had little formal military training, they were excellent marksmen and knew the ways of the woods. Even so, they could not provide the necessary protection, and the Indians, provoked by the

The Indians did not obligingly mass their armies in the open field in neat platoons, but were consummate guerrilla fighters who kept to the woods in small bands. It was unusual to meet them face to face as illustrated here—for the sake of portraiture. *From James Steward,* History of the Discovery of America *(n.d.), Folger Library copy.*

235

King Philip, whose Indian name was Metacomet, Chief of the Wampanoags and son of Massasoit. From him Americans first learned, of grim necessity, to abandon "civilized" warfare for guerrilla tactics, a lesson that has had to be relearned time upon time. This engraving was first published with *The Entertaining History of King Philip's War* by Thomas Church in 1772, wherefore "the costume is no doubt very correctly represented, as the belts and other ornaments worn by King Philip were then to be seen." *From the Folger Library copy of Samuel G. Drake,* History of Boston *(1853).*

French, slaughtered many settlers in the outlying districts in this yet undeclared war.

About the time that Braddock was marching to disaster on the Monongahela, a wily Irishman in New York, William Johnson, who had won the friendship of the Iroquois Indians, was organizing a provincial army at Albany. Johnson had carved out for himself a vast territory in upper New York and had already grown rich from the fur trade with the Six Nations, as the Iroquois Confederation was called. He was determined not to let the French destroy his own prosperity and ruin the colony of New York, and he exerted his personal prestige with both Indians and whites to bring together a force to march against the French. By September he had about three thousand farmers ready to fight. They were an ill-organized and non-descript lot, without uniforms or standard weapons. Every man brought his own squirrel rifle and such ammunition and other weapons as he could find. The Indians were enraged because troops under the French commander, Baron Dieskau, had ambushed and slain some of their chiefs. Johnson's force met the French on the shores of Lake George in late September, 1755. A bloody battle took place. Both sides lost many men, but the French finally were forced to withdraw. Baron Dieskau himself was captured and only Johnson's influence with the Iroquois prevented their torturing him to death. This battle was no victory of consequence, but it helped to prevent the Iroquois from deserting the English, whom they had previously accused of cowardice in the face of the French. Johnson himself was given a knighthood by the King for his prowess.

This representation of the Battle of Lake George is remarkable on several counts. It was drawn by an eyewitness, one Samuel Blodget of Boston, sutler with the English forces. It is the first pictorial record of "Indian fighting" from ambush (compare with the diagram from Barriffe's *Military Discipline*) and the first historical print engraved and published in North America. The running title reads: "A Prospective View *of the* BATTLE *fought near Lake George on the 8th of Sepr. 1755, between 2000* English *with 250 Mohawks . . . & 2500 French & Indians . . . in which the* English *were victorious captivating the* French *Genl. with a Number of his Men killing 700 & putting the rest to flight." From the rare engraving in the Huntington Library.*

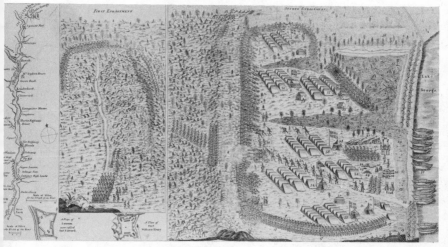

A view of Quebec in the early eighteenth century. The Plains of Abraham, site of Wolfe's decisive victory, are on the high ground to the left. *From the Huntington Library copy of Henry Popple's* Atlas *(1733).*

One reason for some of the disasters that befell the colonies during all of the Indian wars was their complete independence from one another. Each colony tried to shift for itself without regard for the welfare of the others. New York, for example, had a bad record of trading guns and rum with Indians who later used their weapons against other English colonies. The Philadelphia Quakers steadfastly refused to vote money for warfare or to authorize military activities against the common enemies of the colonies. Indians made raids within fifty miles of Philadelphia and scalped many a Pennsylvania settler who had a right to expect some protection from the colonial authorities. When the Governor and Council of Pennsylvania finally went to war against the Indians, many Quakers resigned from the government in protest against this action which went against their religion.

The British sent troops to the colonies, but they were insufficient for the task. Furthermore, the British regulars and the colonial militia disliked each other thoroughly. The regulars thought the militia were undisciplined country bumpkins; the militia thought the regulars were arrogant, high-handed, and ignorant of the way fighting had to be done in the wilderness. Regular British officers, who treated colonial officers with scant respect, were often incompetents who, in accordance with the practice of the time, had bought their commissions.

By the year 1756 a world war was raging, and, as always in the eighteenth century—and later—this continent was involved. The war was known in Europe as the Seven Years' War, but over here, where fighting broke out before the general conflagration in Europe, it has always been called the French and Indian War. The outlook for the colonies in 1756 was dark and gloomy. One of the less competent of British generals was John Campbell, the Earl of Loudon, who was sent to command the British troops. He alienated the colonials by his blustering and dictatorial manner and forfeited their respect by his poor generalship. Pitted against him was a brilliant French general, the Marquis de Montcalm. Under his command the French captured Fort Oswego and established themselves south of

Wolfe's decisive capture of Quebec, September, 1759. The two commanding generals, Wolfe and Montcalm, died within a few minutes of each other. *From the Huntington Library copy of* The London Magazine, *1760.*

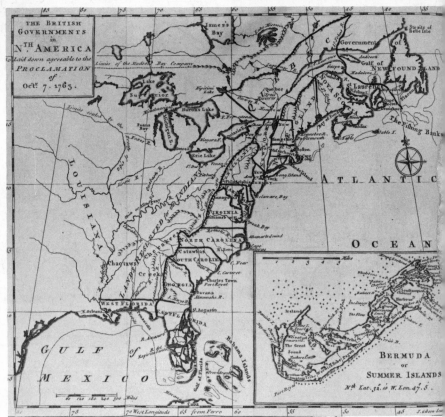

Map of the British possessions in North America as established by the Treaty of Paris, 1763. Note the "Lands Reserved for the Indians" beyond the Proclamation Line along the ridge of the Allegheny Mountains. *From the Huntington Library copy of* The Gentleman's Magazine *for October, 1763.*

Lake Ontario. They also captured Fort William Henry on Lake George and allowed their Indian allies to massacre the New England troops whom they had taken. Loudon was called home and the British sent over another commander, Major General James Abercromby, an even greater disaster than Loudon. It was Abercromby who in July, 1758, led an army of approximately 15,000 troops against the French at Fort Ticonderoga at the southern end of Lake Champlain and lost 2,000 men in the first attack. He had neglected to wait for his artillery to blast

240

an opening for his infantry but had ordered his soldiers to crawl through a barricade of sharpened logs to attack the fort's defenders. After this slaughter, Abercromby was forced to withdraw.

The defeat in front of Ticonderoga, however, marked an end of uninterrupted French victories. The British government, shocked by defeats in all parts of the world, had in the meantime made William Pitt prime minister. Pitt weeded out incompetent officers in the army and navy and was the architect of victories that followed this shake-up. For commander in America, he sent over Lord Jeffrey Amherst, who had as his second-in-command General James Wolfe, a brilliant young officer who loved literature as much as he did military tactics and who proved his prowess on more than one battlefield. Before the year 1758 was over, the British had driven the French from their out-

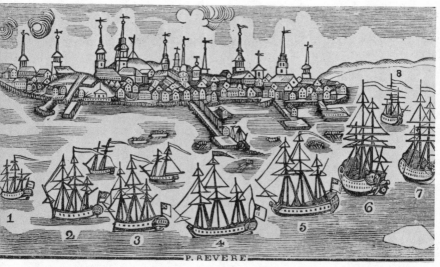

Not long after the Proclamation Line was drawn on the map of 1763, colonial New Englanders were displeased by the arrival of British troops in Boston Harbor. This reproduction of an engraving by Paul Revere was "very exactly copied from *Edes and Gill's North American Almanack and Massachusetts Register* for the year 1770." The title in the Almanac read: "Prospective View of the Town of Boston, the Capital of New England; and of the Landing of Troops in the Year 1768, in consequence of Letters from Gov. Bernard, the Commissioners, etc. to the British Ministry." *From Samuel G. Drake,* History of Boston *(1853), Folger Library copy.*

posts on Lake Ontario and in the Ohio Valley. With the help of the navy, they had also once more taken the fortress of Louisbourg.

From dismal defeat in 1756–57, the British had retrieved their fortunes, and the hazards of slaughter and destruction on the colonial frontiers had diminished. The greatest victory of all came in mid-September, 1759, when General Wolfe led the final assault upon Quebec, which the British had besieged since the end of June. Wolfe personally conducted his troops along a steep hidden path to bring them to a field known as the Plains of Abraham, opposite the weakest defenses of Quebec. In the ensuing attack both Wolfe and Montcalm were mortally wounded, but the British had captured the last of the great French fortresses defending Canada. Although the French army fell back to Montreal and held out for another year, in September, 1760, they finally surrendered to General Amherst.

The peace was confirmed in 1763 by the Treaty of Paris, by the terms of which France ceded all of her North American possessions to Great Britain except two tiny islands, Saint Pierre and Miquelon, off the coast of Newfoundland. Britain magnanimously allowed the French to keep these islands so that her fishermen could dry their nets and cure their fish under their own flag.

The long wars waged by the European powers throughout most of the eighteenth century had all involved the American colonies. Military duties became an accepted fact of everyday life for the colonists. Thousands of young men had served in some capacity in the militia. Many had held commissions and had learned the responsibilities of commanding troops in battle. George Washington was one of many who gained military experience in the French and Indian War that he would later put to good use in the War of Independence.

When the Peace of Paris was proclaimed in 1763, the

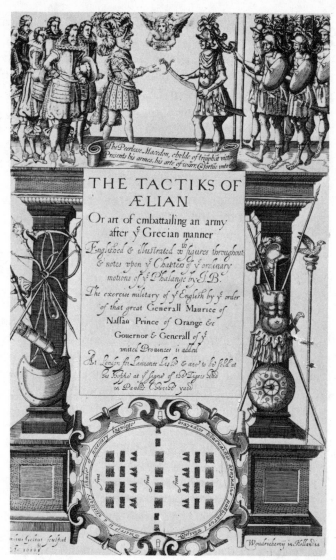

Title page of John Bingham's translation of *The Tactics of Aelian* (1616), one of the military books frequently found in colonial libraries. The Renaissance had inspired study of the Ancients and here Alexander the Great is shown symbolically lending his sword to a modern commander. *From the Folger Library copy.*

future looked bright for the British Empire. Great Britain had been victorious in Europe, in India, and in America. All she had to do now was to pay for the war, consolidate the empire, and reap the profits of world victory. Armchair generals and politicians in London set about putting the empire in order. It seemed to them logical and just that the American colonies should help pay the expenses of maintaining a military force on their side of the Atlantic, and that taxes should be levied upon them for this purpose. Politicians, deeply involved in the fur trade, also thought it desirable to restrain American colonists from encroaching upon the Indians' hunting grounds lest the profitable traffic in skins and furs be disturbed. All this seemed clear and sensible to the heads of the British government, comfortably warming their feet before coal fires in Whitehall.

The decisions in London were not pleasing to the colonials. They had already borne a heavy burden during the wars. Many colonials had lost their lives as soldiers; many more—men, women, and children—had died on the frontiers from Indian arrows and tomahawks. Survivors of the wars did not receive the news of prospective taxation to maintain a standing army of British regulars with favor. Worse still was the injustice, in their opinion, of the Proclamation Line drawn along the ridge of the Allegheny Mountains by the authorities in London to keep white settlers from pushing beyond the mountains into Indian territory. Already white hunters, trappers, traders, and some settlers had crossed the mountains and received a vision of the Great West beyond. They would not willingly allow a few politicians in London to keep them out of the Promised Land. Furthermore, some of the older colonies, Virginia, for example, by their charters claimed land all the way across the continent to the Pacific, though of course this land was as yet unexplored and unknown. They were not willing for the British government in London to eliminate their claims, vague though they might be. Too many speculators had already bought land in the West.

To frontiersmen pushing into the West, the Proclamation Line of 1763 was of far less concern than the hostility of Indians whom they encountered. No actual boundary line existed on the crest of the mountains. The Proclamation Line was merely a mark on a map. But Indians were real and dangerous. In 1763, when in theory peace had come to the colonies, a vicious Indian war broke out on the frontier. It was led by an Indian chief known as Pontiac, who organized a confederation of tribes and attempted to drive the white men back beyond the mountains. In this effort, the Indians were almost successful, for they captured all the white men's outposts in the Northwest except Detroit. The colonial governments could not agree on any concerted action. Though the settlers on the western borders of Pennsylvania suffered more than others, that colony as usual was dilatory about contributing to its defense. After more than a year, British regulars brought the Indians to bay and established an uneasy peace on the western frontier.

Despite the hostility of Indian tribes, the push to the West continued. No authority could keep adventurous white men from penetrating the Indians' territory and taking such land as they could defend. Greed and courage combined to induce settlers to push westward. The movement would gather force until Americans had occupied the entire land to the Pacific Ocean. The settlement of the Atlantic colonies provided the beachhead from which thousands of immigrants would swarm into the interior in the generations to come.

Suggested Readings

[Many of the works in the following list provide information for several of the chapters. Rather than repeat titles under each chapter, the reading list is given for the book as a whole. Some titles will be explicit enough to indicate specific chapters to which they apply.]

Alvord, Clarence W. and Lee Bidgood, *The First Explorations of the Trans-Allegheny Region by the Virginians, 1650–1674.* Cleveland, 1912.

Ashburn, P. M., *The Ranks of Death: A Medical History of the Conquest of America.* New York, 1947.

Bailyn, Bernard, *The New England Merchants in the Seventeenth Century.* Cambridge, Mass., 1955.

Baxter, W. T., *The House of Hancock: Business in Boston, 1724–1775.* Cambridge, Mass., 1945.

Bell, Douglas, *Elizabethan Seamen.* London, 1936.

Bradford, William, *Of Plymouth Plantation.* Ed. by Samuel E. Morison. New York, 1952.

Bridenbaugh, Carl, *The Colonial Craftsman.* New York, 1950.
——— *Cities in the Wilderness, The First Century of Urban Life in America.* New York, 1938; 2nd ed., 1954.
——— *Cities in Revolt, Urban Life in America, 1743–1770.* New York, 1955.

Byrd, William, *The Secret Diary of William Byrd of Westover, 1709–1712*. Ed. by Louis B. Wright and Marion Tinling. Richmond, Va., 1941.

—— *Another Secret Diary . . . , 1739–1741*. Ed. by Maude H. Woodfin and Marion Tinling. Richmond, Va., 1942.

—— *The London Diary, 1717–1721*. Ed. by Louis B. Wright and Marion Tinling. New York, 1958.

—— *The Great American Gentleman* (abridgment of *Diary* of 1709–1712). Ed. by Louis B. Wright and Marion Tinling. New York, 1962.

Dunaway, Wayland F., *The Scotch-Irish of Colonial Pennsylvania*. Chapel Hill, N. C., 1944.

Franklin, Benjamin, *Autobiography*. Ed. by Max Farrand. Berkeley, Calif., 1949. (Many other editions available.)

—— *Poor Richard's Almanac*. Peter Pauper Press, n.d.

Hedges, James B., *The Browns of Providence Plantation: The Colonial Years*. Cambridge, Mass., 1952.

The History of Yankee Whaling. By the editors of *American Heritage*. New York, 1959.

The Journal of John Harrower, an Indentured Servant in the Colony of Virginia, 1773–1776. Ed. by Edward M. Riley. Williamsburg, Va., 1963.

The Journal of Philip Vickers Fithian. Ed. by Hunter D. Farish. Williamsburg, Va., 1943.

Leach, Douglas E., *Flintlock and Tomahawk: New England in King Philip's War*. New York, 1958.

Marcus, G. J., *A Naval History of England: The Formative Years*. Boston, 1961.

Middleton, Arthur P., *Tobacco Coast: A Maritime History of the Chesapeake Bay in the Colonial Era*. Newport News, Va., 1953.

Morgan, Edmund S., *The Puritan Dilemma: The Story of John Winthrop*. Boston, 1958.

—— *Virginians at Home: Family Life in the Eighteenth Century*. Williamsburg, Va., 1952.

—— *The Puritan Family*. Boston, 1944.

Morison, Samuel Eliot, *Builders of the Bay Colony*. Boston, 1930.

—— *Intellectual Life of Colonial New England*. New York, 1956.

Morris, Richard B., *Government and Labor in Early America*. New York, 1946.

Nettels, Curtis P., *The Roots of American Civilization.* New York, 1945; new ed., 1963.

Parry, J. H., *Europe and a Wider World, 1415–1715.* London, 1949.

Peckham, Howard A., *Captured by Indians: True Tales of Pioneer Survivors.* New Brunswick, 1954.

Penrose, Boies, *Tudor and Stuart Voyaging.* Folger Booklets on Tudor and Stuart Civilization, distributed by Cornell University Press, Ithaca, N. Y., 1962.

————— *Travel and Discovery in the Renaissance.* Cambridge, Mass., 1952.

Peterson, Harold L., *Arms and Armor in Colonial America, 1526–1783.* Harrisburg, Pa., 1956.

Quinn, David B., *Raleigh and the British Empire.* London, 1947.

Simpson, Alan, *Puritanism in Old and New England.* Chicago, 1956.

Smith, Abbot E., *Colonists in Bondage: White Servitude and Convict Labor in America, 1607–1776.* Chapel Hill, N. C., 1947.

Smith, Bradford, *Captain John Smith, His Life and Legend.* Philadelphia, 1953.

Smith, John, *The General History of Virginia, New England and the Summer Isles.* First printed, 1624; 2 vols., Glasgow, 1907.

Spruill, Julia Cherry, *Women's Life and Work in the Southern Colonies.* Chapel Hill, N. C., 1938.

Stackpole, Edouard, *Sea-Hunters: The New England Whalemen during Two Centuries.* Philadelphia, 1953.

Sweet, William Warren, *Religion in Colonial America.* New York, 1949.

Tolles, Frederick B., *Meeting House and Counting House: The Quaker Merchants of Colonial Philadelphia.* Chapel Hill, N. C., 1948.

Tunis, Edwin, *Colonial Living.* Cleveland and New York, 1957.

Vandiver, Clarence, *The Fur Trade and Early Western Exploration.* Cleveland, 1929.

Van Doren, Carl, *Benjamin Franklin.* New York, 1938.

Wertenbaker, Thomas J., *The Founding of American Civilization.* 3 volumes, New York, 1938–47.

Williamson, James A., *The Ocean in English History.* Oxford, 1941.

———— *The Tudor Age*. London, 1953.

———— *The Age of Drake*. London, 1938.

Wright, Louis B., *The Atlantic Frontier*. New York, 1951; reissued by the Cornell University Press, 1959.

———— *The Cultural Life of the American Colonies, 1607–1763*. New York, 1957.

———— *The First Gentlemen of Virginia*. San Marino, Calif., 1940; reissued, 1949.

———— *The Dream of Prosperity in Colonial America*. New York, 1965.

Wrong, George M., *The Conquest of New France. A Chronicle of the Colonial Wars*. New Haven, Conn., 1918.

Further Readings

Notestein, Wallace, *The English People on the Eve of the Colonisation*. London, 1954.

Parry, J. H., *The Age of Reconnaissance*. London, 1963.

Simpson, Alan, *Puritanism in Old and New England*. London, 1955.

Index

253

The Author

LOUIS B. WRIGHT has been the Director of the Folger Shakespeare Library in Washington, D. C., since 1948. Before then he was successively an instructor, assistant professor, and associate professor of English at the University of North Carolina, where he also took his graduate degrees. As a member of the Permanent Research Group of the Huntington Library (1932–1948), Dr. Wright was primarily concerned with research in the field of the English Renaissance and American civilization of the colonial period. Much of his research there led to his writing over fifty articles and monographs and over twenty books, many dealing with the colonial period.

Dr. Wright's stature as scholar and author is well-recognized, for he has been the recipient of over twenty honorary degrees from universities here and abroad and a member of various advisory boards in the arts and letters field.